Through God-Colored Glasses

Our world through God-colored glasses for Christians and explorers of Christian spirituality

GREG JANUSZ

Trustworthy Communications, LLC
Ann Arbor

See *god-colored.com* for errata and other information.

Published by Trustworthy Communications, LLC

Copyright © 2009 and 2014 (version 1.0.1) by Greg Janusz
All rights reserved.

Scripture text identified with *NIV* is from the New International Version, Copyright © 1973, 1978, 1984 by International Bible Society (as accessed by http://www.biblegateway.com, November, 2007 through February, 2008)

ISBN 978-0-9822633-0-3

Cover photograph Copyright © 2009 by Greg Janusz

To the Lord, who has
shown me many things
that prophets and kings
longed to see, but did
not see.

To Mom and Dad,
For a lifetime of
support.

Table of Contents

Foreward v
Preface vii
Glossary ix
Introduction xi

Part I
1 Is God Real? 1
2 Who Is God 3
3 The Bible 6
4 How Accurate Is The Bible? 9
5 Which Bible Translation Is Best? 11
6 Need For Forgiveness 13
7 The Great And Terrible Day 15
8 Customize Your Religion 17
9 Inerrancy Or Bust 20
10 Can So Many People Be Wrong? 24
11 Understanding 26
12 Bible Study 28
13 What Is Prayer? 30
14 What Should I Pray? 32

Part II
15 Ghosts and Skepticism 37

16	Argument and Proof	39
17	Extraterrestrial Life	42
18	Equality	45
19	God and Country	48
20	Family Priorities	51
21	The Goddess	53
22	Inherent Value	56
23	Who You Are: Your Greatness	59
24	Glorious Submission	61
25	Free Will vs. Predestination	63
26	Magic and Harry Potter	65
27	In the Name of Jesus Christ	69
28	Wealth and Claiming Verses	72
29	The Real Satan	75
30	Can Satan Read My Mind?	77
31	The Slipperiest Deceptions	80
32	Christian Cults and Cliques	83
33	Jesus, The Fulfillment of the Law	88
34	Did God Really Command the Israelites to Kill Children and Infants?	92
35	Pointing A Gun	96
36	Euthanasia and Suicide	98
37	Adam's vs. Eve's Sin	101
38	Authority, Power, and Responsibility	105
39	Homosexuals	108
40	Leadership Responsibility	112
41	The Good News	115
42	Two Kinds of Faith	117
43	The Cross	121
44	Salvation	124
45	The Personal Relationship	127
46	What Is Faith, Really?	130
47	Little Gods	138
48	Sin	141
49	The Ancestral Connection	143
50	The Community Connection	147
51	Conception	152
52	Atheism, The New Religion	155
53	Such Pain and Suffering	158

| 54 | God: Person or Machine? | 161 |
| 55 | Outthinking the Bible | 164 |

Part III

56	Cycle of the Spirit	171
57	Death	174
58	Fear	177
59	Life	182
60	Potent Human Spiritual Power	185
61	Time Is Short	188
62	You Can Take It With You	190
63	The Master Plan	192
64	Discerning the Genuine	194
65	The End Times, For Us	197

About The Author 203

Foreward

The most important thing about *Through God Colored Glasses* is that it offers hope for everyone. Hope is a word especially dear to its author, Greg Janusz. The authenticity of his experience makes the book powerful for us and for him!

Personal worth has long been Greg's theme; here he shares the way to find it. As a result, he has taken on this life-changing, tough assignment as a road map of sorts to personal worth through personal relationship.

Greg left a job in the technology sector and spent time studying, thinking, and spending time with family. The result of this personal time is a stronger sense of purpose and mission.

This book is not a theological treatise; it is rather a way of viewing the world and the God who created it. It is must reading for all who desire to live a life of personal meaning in a world gone mad. It leads to a path of freedom where all can be who they were really meant to be.

>Dr. JoLynn Gower
>Director and Scholar in Residence,
>Christian Resource Center, Champaign, IL
>Adult Christian Education Coordinator,
>Assemblies of God Church in Champaign, IL
>January, 2009

Preface

This book is written for both Christians who want to fill gaps in their understanding of their faith, and non-Christians who are interested in understanding what Christianity is about with more than the usual depth. Readers who believe that the hundreds of millions of Christians have a rational reason for their faith will get quite a lot out of this book. For someone who is leaning toward the belief that faith in that which can not be seen is irrational, it may be more profitable to read a book on Christian *apologetics*—a more directed defense of the faith.

The explanations are written so that new Christians should understand most of the content, and also so long-time Christians will find a fresh perspective or new thoughts on familiar topics.

It is only fair to explain in advance that the author believes the 66 books and letters that comprise the mainstream Protestant Bible are all *God-breathed*. That is a way of both saying the people that wrote the contents were inspired by God and also that God had such a measure of control as to have selected every word.

The style of writing for this book is that of someone who

believes the Biblical claims of Jesus Christ and has had many experiences consistent with the teachings of the Bible—the stuff upon which faith is built. It would be too wordy to preface each concept with *If God were real...* There is no wording—nor anything else—in this book that is meant to offend. The manner of the writing simply reflects the author's faith, and the contents of the book reflects the kinds of questions that the author has found Christians have.

Glossary

Charismatic.   In the Christian world, a Charismatic Christian is one that believes God still works miraculously through his children as described in 1 Corinthians chapters 12 and 14.

Law.   The capitalized version of *law* refers to the hundreds of commands that God gave the Israelites through Moses. Sometimes this is called the Law of Moses or Mosaic Law. The Law was given to the Israelites to reveal their sins to them and hence to enable them to seek forgiveness for, and be forgiven of, their violations. The Law also contains directions on how to honor God. Christians are no longer under the supervision of the Law (Jesus fulfilled all the requirements of the Law for us), but it is valuable revelation of God's nature, which followers of Jesus Christ will be interested in.

repent.   To change one's mind to agreement with God after learning what God's command is concerning a matter.

righteous.   Because it is a good memory aid, this is often explained as *being right with God*. It is the legal condition a Christian is in once his sins have been forgiven through faith in Jesus Christ. His destination upon death is then to be with Jesus. *Righteous* is also a word used to describe going about one's life in a way that pleases God.

Introduction

The topics (chapters) of this book are roughly arranged in increasing spiritual depth. If the reader finds the first few chapters too trivial, he might skip to Part II. However, some of the material later in the book builds on statements made earlier in the book and it is benficial to start at the beginning.

Most chapters are quite short and encompass one main concept. One can turn to almost any chapter and understand it without having read anything else in the book.

It is the author's hope that readers will have an open mind to the possibility that the contents of this book represent an accurate understanding of God as revealed through the Bible. There is a reason that the Bible has been the most studied book of all time. Not only does it signify a neediness in people that leads them to seek God, but also an avenue to God that has been successful.

It is also the author's hope that those that have been hurt by the Christian church—or those that disagree with the church—will draw a distinction between members of the church and God in their minds. God is perfectly loving, but individuals in the church are oftentimes just trying to survive the troubles of life, and are not necessarily close to successfully reflecting God's attitude and nature. No matter how gentle and wise Christian leaders are, they remain imperfect and make mistakes, sometimes serious ones. God loves those that have walked with him for many years no more than new Christians or even non-Christians, but he deals with each differently, according to his or her needs. I pray he will meet you at your point of need through this book

Part I

1 Is God Real?

God communicates with those who have chosen to follow him and be obedient to him. God left us an important passage about his presence in John 14:15-27. Note the latter part of verse 21 (NIV): *He who loves me will be loved by my Father, and I too will love him and show myself to him.*

There will always be people who argue God does not exist. They believe they have the same information about God as everyone else. In fact, God does not reveal himself to everyone, even though he is near enough to be found by anyone.[1]

Ever since the fall of man in the garden of Eden, God's plan has been the forgiveness of the sins of people and restoring them into right relationship with him. This is not accomplished by God revealing himself to the world. Salvation comes by *faith*, not sight, in Jesus Christ.[2] Some manner of faith in God always precedes or accompanies revelation of God.

Therefore, God's plan of salvation is dependent on his follow-

---

[1] Acts 17:27
[2] John 3:16, Romans 1:16-17, Ephesians 2:8

ers—his children. In John 17:20-23 (NIV), Jesus prays to God the Father: *"...I pray also for those who will believe in me through their message, that all of them may be one... May they also be in us so that the world may believe that you have sent me. ...May they be brought to complete unity to let the world know that you sent me and have loved them even as you have loved me."*

Some would say Christians as a whole are not doing a very good job with their responsibility of unity[3], however, many are fulfilling God's plan of salvation that is described in Romans 4:10-15 and other places.

While evidence can be found everywhere of God's existence[4], it is usually through believing what a Christian has to say that the path toward God is started. Perhaps you know one who is honest and persists in her claims about her experiences of Jesus Christ. **Note the difference between what someone says he *believes* and what he says he has *seen* or *experienced*.** Paul evangelized the Corinthian church with a demonstration of God's power so their faith would not just rest on Paul's words[5]. If one is willing to accept God as he is and follow him, he should pray that to God and start following, but he should not expect much if he does not mean it.[6]

---

3   1 Corinthians 6:6, also the variety of present day disagreements that divide Christians
4   Romans 1:19-20
5   1 Corinthians 2:4-5
6   Luke 16:31, James 1:6-7

2   Who Is God

When we first pick up a Bible, it can appear to be a book with many loosely connected historical narrations. We may be able to see how some of them are connected to each other, but most do not really have an obvious relationship.

God gave us the Bible because he wanted, and still wants, to reveal himself and his love to all people. He wants people to know who is he is so they can decide whether to follow his ways or not. He reveals the advantages of following him and the disadvantages of not following him—as well as what to do to follow him. Rather than having a concise factual list about himself, he chose the more accurate, effective, and timeless method of revealing himself through narratives of interactions he had with individuals, families, and communities.

To know who God is, a great place to start is to read what he said about himself in Exodus 34:5-7 (NIV, bold and text in brackets added): *Then the LORD came down in the cloud and stood there with him and proclaimed his name, the LORD. And he passed in front of Moses, proclaiming, "The LORD, the LORD,* *the **compassionate** and **gracious** God, **slow to anger, abounding in love and faithfulness, maintaining love to thousands** [of generations], and **forgiving wickedness, rebellion and sin. Yet he does not leave the guilty unpunished; he punishes the children and their children for the sin of the fathers** to the third and fourth generation."*

Throughout the Bible we see this list affirmed. It really is a good, concise list, but God is so much more than can be understood through this small number of words. In spite of having what we now call the Old Testament, mankind of two thousand years ago still needed God to come to earth and give us personal instruction. He did just that as Jesus Christ. For about three and a half years, Jesus made disciples and taught them before he completed all the work that he needed to do, and then he returned to heaven.

Because Jesus is God in human form[7], the accounts of his words and behavior are especially valuable and can be found in the first four books of the New Testament. They are called the *gospels*: Matthew, Mark, Luke, and John.

The first book of the Bible, Genesis, gives an account of God creating the universe, and then narrations of some of the first people alive interacting with God. The minimum number of books one should read is, arguably, three: Genesis and John and one other gospel. However, if you want to know who God is, you will gain different knowledge and insight from every part of the Bible.

The trick to grasping a book as big as the Bible is to first strive to understand the timeline of major events, then it is easier to understand how each book fits into the big picture. About the

---
7   John 3:13, Colossians 1:15, Hebrews 1:3

first 70% of the Bible is the *Old Testament* (OT) and mostly has to do with the often rebellious Jewish people, through whom God revealed himself to the world. The OT covers people and events prior to 2000 bc through Jesus' birth around 6 bc.

The last 30% of the Bible, the *New Testament* (NT), covers Jesus' birth through the end of his life around 30 ad, and then mainly letters between teachers God had taught and churches trying to understand what he taught. The books of the NT were all finished by about 95 ad. The last book of the Bible, Revelation, was the last book written. Part of it tells us about God's coming kingdom. For the follower of Jesus Christ, it is an exciting book of hope of what lies ahead.

3   The Bible

The Bible is a collection of writings by more than 35 authors who lived between 1500 bc and 100 ad. Each of these writings is usually referred to as a book of the Bible. Some of the books are epistles (letters) written to a specific person or group of people.

All the books in the Bible have several things in common:

- They are internally consistent. No valid idea about God in one of the books contradicts a valid idea about God in any of the other books. (There are *apparent contradictions* that can be explained.) One of the fundamentals of the Christian faith is that God's nature does not change. Even though God revealed himself through people who lived more than 1500 years apart, the revelations about God are consistent.

- God chose every word and letter that was originally written down. No part of the Bible originated with a human. (The copies we have of the originals are extremely accurate as demonstrated by the science of textual criticism. See also *How Accurate Is The Bible?*)

- They are the books of the *canon*, that is, they are the books the church has officially approved as being God-breathed. Different Christian denominations have different books for their canon. E.g., the Roman Catholic canon has a few more books than the Protestant canon. All of the major Christian denominations (which includes Catholics) have the Protestant canon's 66 books.

The Bible's purpose is to reveal God to us, and as part of that revelation, to know God's love for us and to know ourselves. When reading any section of the Bible it is important to consider why God included it. It is easy to get sidetracked and start reading the Bible with a wrong perspective—which will interfere with us interpreting the Bible correctly.

For example, it is not very difficult to conclude that the New Testament contains the *new set of rules* for Christians to live by—having replaced the Old Testament Law. However, that view is from a wrong perspective. The right perspective requires a foundation of knowing God's love, grace, and what it means that he purchased *freedom from rules* for us.

The Bible reveals God to us through his interaction with people who lived in the past. Necessarily the Bible contains quite a bit of history. But the purpose for a passage may be complete when God has revealed what he wanted to about himself—not when the history has been explained in detail.

In its original form, the Bible did not have any chapter or verse numbers. These were added later as an aid in referring to specific passages. The form citations take is to first name the book of the Bible, which is often abbreviated. Some books start with a number because there is more than one book with the same name. *1 Corinthians* is the first letter from the apostle Paul to the church in Corinth. *2 Corinthians* is the second letter from Paul to the Corinthian church. Note also that *John* is a different book than *1 John*.

What follows is usually a chapter number, then a colon, then a verse number within that chapter. *1 Cor. 2:3* refers to the third verse in the second chapter of the book of 1 Corinthians. *Rom. 8:1-27* refers to the first 27 verses in chapter 8 of the book of Romans. *Rom. 3-8* refers to *chapters* 3 through 8 (inclusive) of the book of Romans.

When citing verses from any of the three books in the Bible that are only one chapter long (*Obadiah, Philemon, and Jude*), the chapter number is left out. *Ob. 1-10* refers to the first 10 verses in the only chapter of the book of Obadiah.

See also *Who Is God?*

4   How Accurate Is The Bible?

A branch of philology called *textual criticism* is the study of documents and fragments of documents to determine the wording of their original texts. This field of study has produced for us accurate renditions of Shakespeare's works, Plato's Republic, Homer's Iliad, and the Bible. Due to deterioration of the writing material and ink of ancient times, the original manuscripts of these works are gone. We only have copies and copies of copies.

An examination of ancient manuscripts reveals differences between copies of the same text. This is primarily the result of having to copy documents by hand before the rise of the use of the printing press in the mid 1400s. Textual criticism addresses how to resolve such differences.

Fragments and copies of the New Testament of the Bible have been preserved in 5,300 Greek manuscripts, 10,000 Latin manuscripts, and 9,300 manuscripts in other languages.[8] The oldest of these copies date to 50 to 250 years after the original was written. (The oldest copies of the *Republic* and *Iliad* are from about 1,000 years after the originals were written.)

Not all ancient manuscripts are fragments. The discovery of the Dead Sea Scrolls in 1947 yielded a full copy of the Book of Isaiah that the University of Arizona carbon-dated to between 335 bc and 122 bc.[9]

The scholarship of textual criticism gives us the confidence we have in the accuracy of the widely accepted renditions of the Bible in its original languages (Hebrew and Aramaic for the Old Testament and Greek for the New Testament). Places in the Bible that scholars did not resolve into a single meaning will have a footnote. In the New International Version the footnote begins with *Some manuscripts* and other translations say *the NU text reads*. See Matthew 5:22 and Romans 11:31 for examples.

The amount of disputed Biblical text is extremely small as one can see by flipping through a Bible looking for these footnotes. The only substantial passages are Mark 16:9-20 and John 7:53 – 8:11.

Translators then use these accurate, compiled original texts to create the modern language translations of the Bible (such as into English).

See also *Which Bible Translation Is Best?*

---

8   http://en.wikipedia.org/wiki/Textual_criticism (accessed December 31, 2007). The author has seen similar numbers from other sources.

9   *New Radiocarbon Age Dates for Dead Sea Scrolls Agree With Paleographic Dates,* University of Arizona Department of Physics. http://www.physics.arizona.edu/physics/public/dead-sea.html (accessed December 31, 2007)

5 Which Bible Translation Is Best?

The Bible was originally written in Koine (common) Greek, Hebrew, and Aramaic. Through the work of scholars, we have accurate versions of the Bible in these original languages. (See also *How Accurate Is the Bible?*) When we start studying the Bible, we want a Bible that has been translated from these original languages into the language we know best.

Bible translators must decide whether they want to translate from the Greek, Hebrew, and Aramaic word-for-word into English or perhaps in a way that conveys the meaning of the passage better for the intended readers. Translating for *dynamic equivalence* is an attempt to translate words, idioms, and grammar into precise English-language equivalents.[10]

For example, in the original Greek in Matthew 16:17, the

---

10 *How To Read The Bible For All Its Worth* by Gordon D. Fee and Douglas Stuart, p. 35, copyright 1993 Zondervan Publishing House, Grand Rapids, Michigan.

apostle Peter's name appears as *Simon Barjona*. Should the translators leave the name as it appears (a literal approach), or use the knowledge that Barjona means *Son of Jonah* to produce the form *Simon son of Jonah* (a more dynamic approach)? The translators could also choose to use *Simon Peter* to reduce the likelihood that a reader might think Simon is a different person than Peter, even though *Peter* is not in the original text at all.

None of these approaches is more correct than another. Which one is chosen depends on what the translators' goals are. The preface in a Bible will describe the translators' chosen approach. Some excellent translations are, in increasing literalness:

- New Living Bible (NLB) – A dynamic equivalent translation of thoughts published by Tyndale using less complex English than the NIV.
- New International Version (NIV) – A popular, high quality dynamic equivalent translation published by Zondervan.
- New American Standard Bible (NASB) – A literal translation published by The Lockman Foundation.

The best way to select a main bible is to read the same passages in different translations and see which one you prefer. Your pastor can suggest other translations if you do not like the ones mentioned above. (There are some bad translations.) You may find that you like one translation for everyday reading and another for more in depth study.

6 Need For Forgiveness

Understanding our sin before God leads us to strongly understand that we need forgiveness from God. Yet sometimes we may wonder why it has to be that way. After all, in spite of all the evil on earth, there is a lot of good. In a country with a fair-minded government, good citizens can live quite happily. They can help the disabled, feed the hungry, and clothe those in need. Why then should death be an event where such people are condemned to eternal punishment?

This thinking is not really far off, but it is the result of having an incomplete view of our world. This story *could* actually end with everyone living happily ever after instead of going to eternal hellfire. The problem with the government and citizens described above is that it leaves God out of the picture.

God is intimately involved in our world. If we began altering our story by including what God is doing one facet at a time, we would start to see a radical transformation of the story. God is heavily involved in *everything*. Not surprisingly, God makes a big impact wherever he is involved. It is his nature. How else could it be with the involvement of the One that created all things, understands how everything works, and why everything works the way it does? Not only is he involved in everything, the only reason anything works in our world is because of God![11]

Amazingly, God is a mixture of being transcendent, far above all understanding, and a being who comes down to our level so that he can interact with us.[12] While he is our God, he is also our Father[13], and our Friend![14] It is impossible to create a story like the one above that is grounded in reality without making God a key figure. Then the effect of him being *God* and his holy presence must be dealt with.

See *Sin*.

---

[11] Acts 17:28, Colossians 1:17
[12] John 16:13-15
[13] Matthew 6:9
[14] John 15:15

7 The Great And Terrible Day

A day will come in which all people that have ever lived and all angels and demons will participate. Most[15] will not be there because they want to be. The day will be both great and terrible. It will echo a day long past that was also great and terrible—the day Jesus suffered on the cross and died.

For all eternity we will be expanding our understanding of the day that God in the flesh, the very source and sustenance of life itself, died. How very different God must be than us to be able to become a paradox of sin and sinlessness. Believe in the infinite power of Goodness, for as a result of this impossibility, sin was destroyed, and sinlessness was victorious. Darkness cannot overcome light. In the presence of light, darkness ceases to exist.

The end of our fallen world and our fallen bodies *must* come. God's holy presence requires it. Woe to the people who choose to remain separate from God during their lives. Only in accepting

---
[15] Matthew 7:13-14

the Goodness of God through The Cross can we approach God. And once we have done so, God gathers us up in his arms and will never drop us. We become children of light, never to fade, but destined to blaze for all eternity.

On the Day of Judgment, we will have to give God an account of all we have said and done on earth. Do you worry what will happen? God tells us what will happen in the Bible. He tells us how to ensure that, for us, the day will be a great day, and not a terrible day.

8 Customize Your Religion

There is a widespread phenomenon of *customizing your religion*. When someone does not like any of the religions he has heard of, he picks and chooses the parts he likes and adopts them as part of his religion. The rest of the ideas are rejected or held at bay because they are believed to be unreasonable (or at best, not understood).

Some people's custom religion is formed by rejecting all ideas that require faith. Some custom religions propose that we are all God, each of us as individuals are God, or that the earth is God. You name it and somebody probably has chosen it as the *most logical or comfortable beliefs for him.*

This approach to a personal religion is tried by many people as part their effort to try to understand and satisfy their spiritual nature. Some stop when they find a set of ideas that are comfortable and others continue into greater depth. For a variety of reasons, people are reluctant to look for the God that *is* instead of the

God that *we want*.

Perhaps the biggest reason is that we know that if we truly discover God as he is, we will have to change our lives—and who wants to change their life into something that inherently acknowledges that he is not in control of his life? Who wants to seek the evidence that requires he submit his life to another?

It is actually not as bad as it sounds. We can decide ahead of time that if God reveals himself as a god who is evil, we will not follow him. Or if he is so arrogant and uncaring as to consider us ants and toys with our lives, we will reject his commands. Something important and wise is that if God proves to not really be a GOD, he is not worth worshiping. In other words, let us choose to only acknowledge God as God if he created our universe, the earth, and ultimately was responsible for creating us. Let us look for a god that is all-knowing and all-powerful.

The God of the Bible, through the apostle Paul, tells us, *For there is no difference between Jew and Gentile—***the same Lord is Lord of all** *and richly blesses all who call on him, for,* **"Everyone who calls on the name of the Lord will be saved."** (Romans 10:12-13, NIV, bold added).

Calling on the name of the Lord must be taken in the context of the surrounding passage, who the writer was, and who his intended readers were—and actually in the context of what is said throughout the entire Bible. Calling on God is part of a process of accepting him as God. The one who calls on the name of the Lord for salvation must be prepared to move forward in what God reveals of himself. There is no such thing as couch potato salvation. God will almost never reveal himself to someone who will not accept him as God and begin moving forward in faith. This is because God loves us and the more knowledge a person has of God, the more responsible he is to respond properly—and the worse his judgment will be if he instead rejects God.[16]

It is a great "bonus" that the God who *is* is not only *not evil*, but he also loves us with infinite love. He is also a God who does not let anyone get away with crime, although sometimes there is a delay before justice is done. Of course, when *we* have committed the crime, we do not want to be punished, but would you really want a God that let criminals get away with their crimes?

---

[16] Luke 12:47

9 Inerrancy Or Bust

What does it mean to suggest that the Bible is *inerrant* (without error)? Does it mean that every sentence taken out of context is true? No, of course not. Understanding the grammatical and cultural context of any sentence in any book is essential to understanding what it means. In fact, even that is not enough. We also need to understand the background of the author and who he believes his readers will be, and what he believes their background to be.

Fortunately, the entire Bible was written by people under God's influence and whose understanding of God was shaped by God, and so we can read their writings as truths about God. We do not have to struggle with every sentence trying to figure out if the author knew what he was talking about or not. But sometimes the author of a book records thoughts other than his own.

In the book of Job, chapters 4 through 25, a man named Eliphaz and two of his friends talk to Job about God, but then in Job 42:7 (NIV), God speaks: *After the LORD had said these things to Job, he said to Eliphaz the Temanite, "I am angry with you and your two friends, because you have not spoken of me what is right, as my servant Job has."*

What Eliphaz and his friends told Job about God, God called *not right*.

There are also portions of the Bible that recount people expressing their thoughts and emotions, but do not necessarily translate directly into true statements about God. King David wrote many of the chapters in the book of Psalms. His character was well shaped by God, and we can read his writings as what it is like to be a Godly human with a very accurate knowledge of what God is like, but his perceptions are still from a human viewpoint.

Inerrancy of the Bible means that God inspired every word in the Bible to be written down and no mistakes were made. While it is necessary to know something of the author's background, what is of first importance is to know that God chose every word as part of what he wanted us to have to learn about him and know him.

Part of the task of the Bible reader is to understand the context of the passages, otherwise incorrect understanding will result, and subsequently, faith in the wrong things.

Another issue that some people grapple with is founded in the idea that some of the Bible is inerrant, but not all of it. However, there are very good reasons to believe that it is all inerrant.

The apostle Peter, one of the three closest people to Jesus when he was on earth, wrote in 2 Peter 3:15-16 (NIV, bold added), *Bear in mind that our Lord's patience means salvation, just as our dear brother Paul also wrote you with the wisdom that God gave him. He writes the same way in all his letters, speaking in them of these matters. His letters contain some things that are hard to understand, which ignorant and unstable people distort,* *as they do the **other Scriptures**, to their own destruction.*

Peter wrote this about 67 ad, a few years *after* the last of the 13 New Testament books that were clearly written by the apostle Paul. It tells us that Peter considered Paul's writings equivalent to the Scriptures of that time (primarily what we call the Old Testament, which were well accepted as God's words).

In Matthew 22:23-33, Jesus explained that God affirmed that the resurrection of the dead was really going to happen because in Exodus 3:6, God used the present tense instead of the past tense when he told Moses, *I **am** the God of Abraham, the God of Isaac, and the God of Jacob.* (Matthew 22:32, NIV, bold added). We see here that Jesus believed this passage of the Old Testament right down to the verb tense that God used.

We also see in many other places that Jesus believed the Old Testament[17] as did the apostle Paul.[18] In Ephesians 2:20, Paul positively affirms that his readers' faith is built on the Old Testament prophets and the *apostles*—the twelve that Jesus selected, some of whom wrote the New Testament books of Matthew, John, 1 John, 2 John, 3 John, Revelation, 1 Peter, and 2 Peter.

Do you see why picking and choosing what you want to believe out of the Bible invalidates most, if not all of the Bible? If you reject a small portion of it, you will simultaneously be discrediting authors or their statements in other parts of the Bible. The foundation of your faith will quickly crumble, and you will be left with doubt about everything in the Bible. Whatever is left will not even remotely resemble Christianity. (See also *Customize Your Religion*.)

A part of the Christian walk is to grow in knowledge and un-

---

17 Matthew 5:17, 26:56, Luke 18:31, 24:25, 27, 44
18 Romans 1:1-2, 3:21, Galatians 4:4, et al.

derstanding of the truth. Deciding to follow Jesus Christ does not instantly grant us a knowledge of, or belief in, the right things. No one need be ashamed of not fully understanding what they think they believe. Some ideas we believe because our pastor preached them as the truth. Some come from our own reading of the Bible. But these are starting points for our faith. If left in that condition our faith will be on shaky ground and will be susceptible to falter or collapse.

Many Christians would say they believe everything in the Bible, in part because they were taught that it was all *God-breathed*.[19] But if then asked if they believed a loving God would ever command genocide, including children and infants, they may be less certain if they believe that.[20] This is a normal part of a growing knowledge and understanding of the Bible and God.

---

19 2 Timothy 3:16
20 See *Did God Really Command the Israelites to Kill Children and Infants?*

10 Can So Many People Be Wrong?

Statistics are published every now and then listing how many people profess to be members of various religions. If you examine the statistics for the whole world, you may find figures roughly similar to these:

Christianity	33%	2.2 billion
Islam (Muslims)	21%	1.4 billion
Athesism and Non-religious	16%	1.1 billion
Hinduism	14%	950 million
Buddhism	6%	400 million
Others	10%	680 million

When considering such large numbers of people, a reasonable reaction is, *Can so many people be wrong?*

Each of the major religions listed above excludes the others by their fundamental beliefs. For example, while Islam recognizes Jesus as a prophet, it rejects the idea that Jesus is the Son of God and hence equal to God—a fundamental part of basic Christian belief. Islam can not remain Islam if it bends enough to accept this basic facet of Christianity.

Even within the broad umbrella of people who call themselves Christians there are denominations that have beliefs that are fundamentally incompatible with other Christian denominations.

Some people believe that God is larger than any individual religion, and that each of these major religions may be a different path to God. However, the same argument applies. Christianity, for example, rejects this possibility so fundamentally[21], that it can not be true if the tenets of Christianity are true.

So, unfortunately, yes, many people are wrong. In fact the only logical conclusion after examining the major religions is that they are all wrong or exactly one of them is right and the rest are wrong. No two of them can be right.

---

21   Exodus 20:22-23, Acts 4:8-12, Galatians 1:8, and *many* other passages.

11 Understanding

The fear of the LORD is the beginning of knowledge, but fools despise wisdom and discipline. (Proverbs 1:7, NIV)

We can find both the obvious and the mysterious in the Book of Proverbs. For example, what does fear (reverence and awe) of God have to do with knowing how to add two numbers together (knowledge)?

The author is convinced that understanding is a result of knowing facts combined with experiences. In other words, we cannot truly understand knowledge we have without experiencing it in some fashion.

One understands something when he can apply what he knows to a variety of situations and derive correct, verifiable conclusions. If one thinks he knows the rules of addition but whenever he add two numbers together he gets the wrong result, obviously he does not know the rules of addition as well as he thought! If someone's knowledge and experiences are extensive on a subject, then we can say that person has *wisdom* pertaining to that matter (presuming he has the self-discipline to apply it).

In the same way, if someone claims to love another, but does not see the fruits of love, then perhaps he does not love them as he thinks he does. (The fruits of love would be observable in the one loving, not the object of his love.) Jesus said, *Greater love has no one than this, that he lay down his life for his friends.* (John 15:13, NIV) He spoke of a very visible and powerful form of love.

Which parts of the Bible do you understand the best? Are they not the parts that speak of matters that you have personally experienced? It is through these parts of the Bible that God reveals himself to you.

As you gradually understand more of the Bible and obey more of the Bible, God reveals himself more to you. Is it any wonder that the essence of being a Christian is found in obedience to God? We are to act on what God wants us to do. How else is he going to reveal himself to us if we do not have the experiences by which we can understand him?[22]

---

22   James 1:22-25

12 Bible Study

If you picked up the Bible on your own and began reading, you may have found it to be largely unintelligible. If you first were exposed to it at a Bible study, you may have felt lost and irredeemably ignorant.

However, there is no reason whatsoever to feel defensive or put down by a lack of Bible knowledge. Not a person walks the earth who understands the whole Bible as applied to his life. Everyone studying the Bible is a Bible student to one degree or another. Allow yourself to switch into a mode of thinking where you accept that you are a student of the Bible and that you will learn from other students who once had zero knowledge of the Bible.

It is important to realize that the direction we are traveling is more important than how far along the path we are. This is true for all spiritual matters, not just learning from the Bible. God has neither pop quizzes nor due dates for our Bible knowledge. We can only live in the present, and he holds us accountable for what we can do in the present. We are allowed to learn at our own pace, and encouraged to set a pace slow enough that we can sustain it for a long time. (This might be quite slow at first!)

Rather than leave you to the inevitable self-comparison when you discover how much other people study the Bible, the author suggests that you dedicate at least 30 focused and uninterrupted minutes per week, not counting the time it takes you to mentally "shift gears." Allow yourself to go over the allotted time if you want to, and allow yourself to increase the number of days per week if you like. Also allow yourself to stop entirely for a season, but try to get back into the habit when you can.

At this amount of Bible study, you may very well run into people who look down on you for how little you read the Bible. It is important to not let anyone steal the freedom you have been given by Jesus Christ.[23] (Please note two big caveats to this freedom: one is that you must not cause anyone else to stumble because they see your freedom,[24] and also that God does expect you to get spiritual guidance from church elders.[25])

Reading the Bible is a much more enjoyable experience when you realize that it is all true and almost all of it provides insight into who God is—who desires to interact with you. It helps you understand how the universe works, who you are (you are great!), and how you fit in to it all.

---

23 1 Corinthians 10:29
24 1 Corinthians 8:9-13, 10:28-29
25 1 Thessalonians 5:12-13, Hebrews 13:17, 1 Peter 5:1-7

13 What Is Prayer?

Prayer is communicating with God. Most commonly, it refers to speaking aloud to God or thinking words and sentences directed to God. Praying to anyone else is not found in the Bible. Fortunately, God is completely approachable and loves to hear your prayers. Before Jesus died and was raised, people needed to go through a *priest* to have access to God. However now all Christians are *priests*[26] from God's perspective and we all have direct access to him.[27]

God knows everything, including everyone's thoughts. Some people find it unnerving that God knows their thoughts, but God respects your privacy. Some people describe God in this context as a *gentleman*. God's compares his presence to a gentle whisper.[28]

Prayer can also be more than just the constructed sentences we speak to God. We use facial expressions, body language, and tone of voice to communicate with other people. God is aware of

---
26 1 Peter 2:5, 9, Revelation 1:6
27 Ephesians 3:12, Hebrews 4:16, 10:19-22
28 1 Kings 19:11-13

What Is Prayer?

all of these and more. Possibly the loudest way we communicate is through our choices and actions. Anything in our life can be considered prayer to God, especially if we do it with the intention that it be received by God.

It is valuable for Christians to develop the habit of regular prayer that includes praising God, repenting of any sins, thanking God for what he has done for us and given us, making requests, and thinking about what we have read in the Bible.

Some examples of prayer in the Bible are:

- Nehemiah's prayer in Nehemiah 1:5-11
- David's prayer in 2 Samuel 7:18-29
- Various chapters in the Book of Psalms
- Jesus' prayer to God the Father in Matthew 6:9-13
- Jesus' prayer to God the Father in John 17

See also Paul's instructions to Timothy about prayer in 1 Timothy 2:1-4.

See also *Potent Human Spiritual Power*.

14 What Should I Pray?

God loves you and is open to anything you want to say to him. If a matter concerns you, then it concerns God.

Some people would suggest that it is appropriate to be respectful or reverent while praying, but it is OK to be emotional with God, too, and sometimes our emotions interfere with our desire to be polite. God would rather you pray to him in a less than perfect mood than to not pray to him.

Knowing how God sees his role in our life and knowing who he is gives us insight into what it is good to pray about. The most important goal of studying the Bible is to get to know God better.

The Lord's Prayer can be viewed as topics to pray about as we seek the Lord to involve himself in our lives and thank him for what he has given us.

Matthew 6:9-13 (NIV)	Topic
Our Father in heaven,	Our relationship to our heavenly father
hallowed be your name,	Reverence to God by all
your kingdom come,	Coming of the Kingdom of God on Earth
your will be done on earth as it is in heaven.	The Lord's desires being fulfilled on Earth
Give us today our daily bread.	What we need from God
Forgive us our debts, as we also have forgiven our debtors.	Our need for forgiveness and our ability to forgive
And lead us not into temptation, but deliver us from the evil one.	Guidance and protection

God loves us as his children, and likes to give us good gifts.[29] Consider what is most important to you and talk to God about it. God is not stingy in granting requests, but he has everyone's long-term good in mind, and may not answer your prayer right away or in the manner you anticipate.

---

29   Luke 11:1-14 especially 11-14, 1 Timothy 6:17, Psalm 37:4

Part II

15 Ghosts and Skepticism

Although angels and demons make many appearances in the Bible, ghosts that haunt places are not found in the Bible. It would be incorrect to try to argue that, therefore, the Bible teaches that ghosts must not exist. The logic behind such an argument is the same as what an Atheist uses to say, *since I have not experienced God, he must not exist*. All it takes is for one person to encounter a real ghost to refute the proposition that ghosts do not exist.

If a person had firmly decided a priori that ghosts do not exist, he must conclude that the claim of the person having encountered the ghost must be a lie or the person must have been hallucinating or deceived in some way. This reasoning can be called anything from *appropriate skepticism* to *close-mindedness.*

What is the difference between a person who believes everything he hears—until proven otherwise, and a person that is skeptical of everything he hears—until it is demonstrated? The believer considers the skeptic close-minded, and the skeptic considers the believer naïve. Neither evaluation is unbiased. The open-minded perspective is that the believer must admit that he might be wrong, unless the evidence meets a certain criteria for belief, and the skeptic must admit entities and events can exist that are outside his experience.

There is a key difference in these two perspectives. The believer can accumulate evidence for his belief over time, whereas, the skeptic must *never* accumulate enough evidence to change his personal criteria for belief. In other words, the believer's faith rests on evidence and the skeptic's faith rests on the lack of evidence. In both cases, the evidence is relative to the person's *personal* criteria for belief. It is possible and quite common for the same evidence to convince one person, but not another. Another key difference is that the believer has experienced both the lack of evidence and sufficient evidence, while the unbeliever has only experienced the lack.

Some unbelievers seem to feel at a disadvantage with their position of lacking evidence, since they know that they have not had all experiences that exist. But there is nothing wrong with him suggesting that he has personally not experienced enough evidence to change his mind and leaving it at that. This is the position *everyone* is in regarding a multitude of life's possible experiences, including those that believe in God.

It is perfectly reasonable for an open-minded Atheist to pray this: *God, if you are really out there, please meet my personal criteria for believing in you enough to accept you as my God.* Persisting in this prayer has value in that it may further a self-examination of if he really means it, or if he really does not want there to be a God. God will answer the prayer for the former, but not usually the latter.

16   Argument and Proof

The apostle Paul instructs his readers to have nothing to do with *foolish and stupid*[30] arguments or *fine-sounding*[31] arguments. He also instructs to avoid foolish arguments because they are *unprofitable and useless.*[32] What is a *foolish* argument? One kind of foolish argument is attempting to *prove* that God is or is not real, or Jesus Christ is or is not the Son of God.

The dictionary may give definitions that equate *proof* with *enough evidence to believe*, but the word *proof* is rarely used that way in religious arguments such as about the existence of God. Usually it is used in such a way as to mean *evidence that cannot be refuted by even the most skeptical person*. This definition allows any other explanation against the proof to seem to be a way to discredit that proof. This is a rather useless definition for

30   2 Timothy 2:23
31   Colossians 2:4
32   Titus 3:9

proof, since there are always unlikely explanations for anything. The dictionary definition is much more useful, but we must realize that sufficient evidence to believe for us might differ from sufficient evidence for someone else.

For example, the *fine-sounding argument* that an all-powerful God of love can not exist because there is so much suffering on earth is based on false assumptions. It presumes that God is a God of love with *our* definition of *love*. It also assumes that if God is not halting all suffering, it must be because he does not have enough power. The possibility he is an all-powerful, loving God with another reason for not stopping all suffering is often not examined sufficiently.

The main reason that *arguments* can be foolish is because they are so *unprofitable and useless* and produce *quarrels*, just as Paul writes. Consider an argument between two people, one for the existence of the God of the Bible, and one against it. One of the people may be better educated or better prepared; one of the people may be a talented debater, or a highly analytical and precisely logical person. One of the two may clearly be the winner of the argument. But nothing about those two individuals' capabilities or their arguments affects the existence of God. The winner of the argument could very well be wrong. Also, the winner of the argument is only the winner *at that time—between the people present*. There are undoubtedly many people on earth who could demolish the arguments of the so-called winner.

Do not confuse this example argument with a *discussion* between an Atheist and a Christian. An argument and a discussion are quite different. A discussion is (ideally) for the improvement of both people. (*Instruction* is for the improvement of primarily one of the people.) In a good discussion, both people are open to learning. They are both open to being wrong about some of their thinking, and open to improving their thinking based on each other's thoughts.

An *argument*, on the other hand, is often primarily an *emotional* interaction. **We are formulating explanations in our minds that will satisfy our emotions.** What is actually happening in an argument is easiest to see when considering two children, one insisting *is* and the other insisting *is not!* Consider the banter: *Is! Is not! IS! IS NOT!* The children are not yet developed enough to create a train of logic to back up their feelings, so all they can do is express their feelings. This can be no different than an argument between adults, except that the adults may have the resources to form *fine-sounding arguments*.

If the goal of having a particular discussion is to convince someone of one's position, the goal is not to *prove* one's position. It is to influence the other person to have *faith* in one's reasoning, experiences, or beliefs. We explore and discuss the evidence of God and Jesus Christ not so their existence can be *proven*, but so that others might gain a measure of *faith* in God. To those who wanted proof, Jesus said they will not get it. They will only have Jesus' message of the need to repent.[33]

---

33 Matthew 12:38-39, 16:1-4, Mark 8:11-13, Luke 11:29-32

17 Extraterrestrial Life

Why do people search for extraterrestrial life? Here on earth, each individual is ignorant of a vast array of living creatures—no one is familiar with them all. If one wanted to study new life, all a person could ask for is here. Perhaps the desire is really to find a foreign form of life that is intelligent enough that we could exchange fresh ideas and learn from each other. But there are so many cultures on earth, it is unlikely that any individual is even passingly familiar with them all. Why not examine one of earth's non-industrial, third-world cultures?

Perhaps some of us have an inborn instinct to do something that no one has done before. Interacting with a non-earthly life in some way would certainly propel the people involved into the limelight—like the first person to climb to the top of the highest mountain in the world.

Many of us certainly have a low esteem for life or see such a huge diversity of life on earth and would find it difficult to believe that humankind on earth is special and unique in the universe.

It may be that we have a sort of motherly instinct and want to help a race of beings prone to the past mistakes of mankind to bypass those errors. Or perhaps it is a combination of the above. We each have a variety of inner needs, and we may feel that the challenges of relating with a completely brand new life would meet our needs—when the challenges on earth have only brought us frustration.

However, the author believes the biggest reason people search for extraterrestrial life is in the hope of finding an older, wiser race of beings that can help us with our problems. A car's bumper sticker has concisely expressed our angst: *Beam me up, Scotty! There's no intelligent life down here!* This sentiment has been expressed through the ages.[34]

Tragic and even horrific activities take place on earth. Who would not want a grandfatherly species to come and put a stop to all of earth's conflicts? They could show us how to stop war, famine, and cancer. Torture, depriving people of their dignity, and maintaining thousands of nuclear weapons could come to an end. The environmental destruction on earth could be fixed and we could be shown ways to be good stewards of the earth.

But if such an alien race came to visit us, is it not possible they might respond with, *Earthlings have the knowledge to solve most of their problems. The problem is that they do not want to follow their own wisdom.*

Indeed, we have the knowledge of how to stop wars—people stop killing each other. We have the knowledge to eliminate nuclear arms, famine, and the degradation of people.

There will always be people that have a different perspective than you that will frustrate your efforts to make a better world for yourself. More to the point, you believe you have the right to

---

[34] 2 Corinthians 5:2-8, Romans 8:23-25, Hebrews 13:14

certain things, and there are other people that disagree. This will always be the case. The only way peace can exist between such people is if they were willing to give up some of their rights for the sake of peace. This willingness is perhaps the single largest component of true *love*.[35]

This is precisely the model of living that Jesus taught and exemplified.[36] Jesus had the right to have the worship of all humans; instead he was an "extraterrestrial life form" that came as a servant[37] to humans and suffered and died for them—the example that he explicitly taught we must follow.[38]

Regarding fellow Christians, Paul echoed Jesus' teaching in 1 Corinthians 6:7 (NIV): *The very fact that you have lawsuits among you means you have been completely defeated already. Why not rather be wronged? Why not rather be cheated?*

---

35 John 15:13
36 Matthew 5:38-42
37 Mark 10:45
38 Luke 9:23

18   Equality

Are you a supporter of equality between the sexes and races? Have you ever been discriminated against? It can feel like violence done to one's personhood. It may make you feel powerless—a similar helplessness as when an authority figure abuses his power and position contrary to what seems right to you. Your gut reaction may be anger or you may feel demeaned. It can feel so *unfair*.

We don't all have equal needs and desires. Wouldn't *special* treatment for everybody be better? Would you be willing to give up being treated equally to be treated as special?

A good start would be to realize that when someone treats *someone else* (i.e., not you) as special they are usually focused on themselves and what they are trying to do so much that they did not intend to show any disrespect to you. Without this foundation of understanding, special treatment for a group of individuals probably cannot be sustained, and may not even get off the ground.

If you work in America today, you have a mix of equal and

special treatment. Maternity leave is rarely offered when neither you nor your spouse gives birth, so those that take maternity leave are being treated *specially*. However, vacation time is usually offered in a way that is consistent for all employees. If you were diagnosed with cancer, would you rather take time off according to your needs or according to a predetermined plan applied equally to everyone?

It is unfortunate that people are put in positions of authority (or elected) without having first experienced the kinds of things that they will require of others. If you were in the armed forces, wouldn't you prefer a commander who had been in the kind of circumstances you are ordered into? If you are in danger of becoming homeless, wouldn't you prefer that your church members and city council members had also been in danger of being homeless at one time? Even so, everyone's experiences are unique to them. Just because you have had major surgery does not mean that you can understand what another person will go through when she experiences major surgery.

Here we discover the value of *wisdom*, which the Bible speaks very highly of.[39] No one can have the experiences that other people have. However, someone that has had *many* similar experiences may gain wisdom which can be applied to someone else's situation. Fortunately for us God has all wisdom, and the result is security for those who listen to him. Proverbs 30:5 (NIV) says, *Every word of God is flawless; he is a shield to those who take refuge in him.*

It's a good thing God doesn't treat us all the same way. We are each created uniquely and special through God's love. He never treats us as if we are someone else. As his children, he calls us to

---

39   Proverbs 2-4, et al.

do the same.

Praise be to the God and Father of our Lord Jesus Christ, the Father of compassion and the God of all comfort, who comforts us in all our troubles, so that we can comfort those in any trouble with the comfort we ourselves have received from God. For just as the sufferings of Christ flow over into our lives, so also through Christ our comfort overflows. (2 Corinthians 1:3-5)

19 God and Country

Americans are among the most blessed people in the world. The excellence of our Constitution and Amendments in protecting freedom is nearly miraculous and affects everybody in one way or another. The wealth of the country affects everybody as well, even the poorest American. The fact that you can find a grocery store nearby where you can buy food if you have a dollar is something that much of the world does not have.

It should be with thanksgiving that we also recognize that we live in a country where we can allow our beliefs to influence our lives without fear of torture or death (usually). Many of the Christians in the world do not have this comfort. Furthermore we can be thankful that our *government's laws* are oriented to protecting our freedom to practice religion. This is exactly what our First Amendment states as ratified in 1791:

Congress shall make no law respecting an establishment of religion, or prohibiting the free exercise thereof; or abridging the freedom of speech, or of the press; or the right of the people peaceably to assemble, and to petition the Government for a re-

dress of grievances.[40]

The author interprets the first clause this way, translating the word *respecting* from what it meant in the English of 1791 ("showing preference for"):

1. Congress is not allowed to make a law that gives preference to a particular religion.
2. Congress is not allowed to make a law that prevents anyone from practicing their religion.

This amendment seems divinely inspired. Does it not provide the exact framework that God wants for us? Forcing someone to be a Christian is loathsome to God. What he wants is an environment where we can know about him and choose to follow him if we choose to. Two things are required for this: knowledge of him and the freedom to choose him. Evangelism as directed by God provides the former and the first amendment provides the latter—although the human heart has the freedom to choose God regardless of a country's laws.

Our legal system provides a way to clarify the meaning of the amendment—with good reason. There is no way to encapsulate an explanation of Congress' relationship to religion for every complex situation that arises through the years in just 16 words. The method for elaborating on the original meaning is done through *case law*, that is, the thinking of the judges involved in specific cases that draw on the first amendment. Subsequent cases can draw on such thinking as a legal elaboration of the first amendment.

---

40   The National Archives. *Bill of Rights.* http://www.archives.gov/national-archives-experience/charters/bill_of_rights.html (accessed: December 4, 2007).

In 1994 Supreme Court Justice David Souter provided such a clarification in one such case. He wrote, *government should not prefer one religion to another, or religion to irreligion.*[41]

The author believes this ruling can also be read to mean that government should not prefer *irreligion to religion.* Unfortunately, there is a massive Atheistic trend to do exactly that infused into most of our politicians—contrary to the protections our laws provide. (See also *Atheism, The New Religion*)

It is important to understand that our laws are meaningless apart from people. In a third world country, laws written on a piece of paper do not mean anything if the head of the army wants to ignore them. Our laws are meaningful and powerful only when we behave in a way that affirms them.

The power of our laws comes from the citizens. This demands citizen (i.e., Christian) participation in our government—in a way that works within our laws. The passages about Joseph in Egypt[42] and the Book of Daniel give us glimpses of Godly men functioning in less-than-ideal governments. How much easier it should be for Christians to participate in American government whose laws protect such involvement.

---

41   FindLaw. *Board of Education of Kiryas Joel Village School District v. Grumet, 512 U.S. 687 (1994).* http://caselaw.lp.findlaw.com/scripts/getcase.pl?navby=CASE&court=US&vol=512&page=687. (accessed December 4, 2007)

42   Genesis 37-50.

20 Family Priorities

From the author's understanding of the Bible, these are our life priorities:

1. God
2. Your Spouse
3. Your Children
4. Your Parents[43]
5. The rest of your immediate family
6. Your extended family, other Christians,[44] and doing the work God has given you to do
7. Strangers, your work
8. Yourself

This is a list to help you weigh the importance of complex matters in confusing situations. There is no simple way to view the many responsibilities and opportunities that tug at our lives.

---

43   Mark 7:9-13
44   1 Timothy 5:8

It does not provide you with the justification to do certain things because they have a higher priority than other things.

Your spouse is higher on the list than your children. You are raising your children for the Lord. You are preparing them to live on their own—they will, except for special situations, leave your home eventually, but continue to grow in their relationship with God without you. Your spouse will not—God has joined you with your spouse in obvious as well as mysterious, spiritual ways, until death.

This list does not decide for you whether keeping your boss happy, through whom you support your family, is more important than keeping your spouse happy. That is a complicated situation. This is a just a simple list.

Do not say that because God is on the top of the list, you do not have time on your way to church to stop and help someone in need because they are on the bottom of the list. Do not say that because your spouse is higher on the list than yourself, that you must stay in an abusive marital situation.

This is not a list of priorities to help you order your tasks. If you are out to save the world/strangers, this list does not mean, make sure you have saved items 2-7 first. What it does mean is that you have limited energy, time, and resources. Make sure you allocate those precious commodities in a way that is consistent with good stewardship of what God has given you.

Lastly, you may think that doing God's work is too low on the list, but God set that priority pretty strongly in 1 Timothy 5:8 (NIV): *If anyone does not provide for his relatives, and especially for his immediate family, he has denied the faith and is worse than an unbeliever.*

21   The Goddess

Is it any wonder that people are more comfortable with the idea of a Goddess than a God? Authority has historically, and still primarily, rests in the hands of men. Because males have held most positions of authority and leadership, nearly all abuses of power are from men. Most punishment is carried out by men. Sadly, our church institutions with their mostly male leadership have dealt their share of abuse just like any secular institution. In homes, the father tends to be a more forceful personality than mothers—as well as less outwardly *emotionally* caring. In homes where the father is not present, the mother has obviously been more reliable and faithful.

Mothers historically, and still primarily, have more nurturing and more outwardly caring personalities than fathers. Mothers are generally softer in their interactions with children and more approachable.

Wouldn't it be great if God were a soft personality, an ally whom you could count on to be sympathetic to your difficulties and to comfort you. When you stumbled and hurt yourself, wouldn't you rather have God cry with you knowing how much you hurt and put a bandage on you, rather than explain why it happened and what you did wrong that caused it—and how to avoid it next time?

Fortunately, the God of the Bible fully encompasses what we think of as motherly nature. It is not only man that was made in God's image, *man and woman* were made in God's image. Consider God's description of himself from Exodus 34:6-7. God is:

- compassionate
- gracious
- slow to anger
- abounding in love
- abounding in faithfulness
- faithful in his love to many
- forgives wickedness, rebellion, and sin
- punishes the guilty

The whole of Scripture backs up this concise description of himself that God gives. Even with our sense of male authority warped by the imperfect men of our world, *punishes the guilty* is still the only standout "male" characteristic. All of God's other stated attributes are more easily (or at least equally) attributed to the stereotypical woman than the stereotypical man.

The Old Testament stories of God's many punishments and the New Testament's "rules that we must follow" can easily paint a wrong picture of God. As always Scripture *must* be read in context.

The Old Testament is primarily the revelation of God to people living as they please without regard to God's moral standard. Not surprisingly God's judgments figure heavily into these narratives. There is also much about God's interaction with obedient people, but these present less vivid, and less easily remembered, narratives. (Read Isaiah 40-66.)

The New Testament contains witnesses to Jesus' ministry, along with much instruction for baby Christian churches who have a lot to learn about God. Consider Jesus' words to the churches that are mostly doing well in Ephesians, Colossians, and Revelation 3:7-13. For example, in the Revelation passage, Jesus offers only praise, encouragement, and hope to people who have been obedient in difficult times.

22   Inherent Value

Society and laws in America have a strong emphasis on the *equality* of all people. People who think they are better than others are usually considered sexist, racist, or at the very least, offensively arrogant.

In Biblical times the opposite was true—it was absurd to consider men and women equal, or Jews and non-Jews equal. Jesus came and demonstrated a new value system.[45] The New Testament teaches that no one should be given preferential treatment.[46] Every follower of Christ is made priceless through the indwelling of the Holy Spirit. All are made equal *in Christ*.[47]

Growing up in a culture with kings and slaves had an advantage not available to us: it was easier to understand God's greatness. An understanding of God's greatness from reading the Bible results in a pale understanding compared to living in a time when the king was considered divine and his word was law. You could see the king's army and could experience his justice. You could

---
45   Luke 10:38-42, John 4:4-9
46   James 2:1-10
47   1 Corinthians 12:13, Galatians 3:28, Colossians 3:11

Inherent Value

see his authority backed up by power: both in demanding taxes and in protecting his people. It would have been more meaningful when someone explained, *as much as a king is greater than a slave is God greater than all kings.* Indeed, one of the names of Jesus is *King of kings and Lord of lords.*[48]

The Bible is not a particularly good source of stories about benevolent and great kings. Even David, the most Godly king the Jews ever had, was a man of violence out of necessity.[49]

To explain how great God's love is for each of us, it has been said that if there had only been one person to save, Jesus still would have sacrificed his life and done all he did for that one person.[50] It is true: a single person—you—are that precious to God. In fact, you are worth more than all the money, animals, planets, and stars in the universe combined because of God's love for you.

In the same way, God is worth more than all the people who have ever lived combined. Only God has always existed. Only God has never done wrong. Only God has created everything that we know. When God tells of his greatness, he is not being arrogant. He is blessing us because the truth is precious, and it is in our best interest to understand who we are and who God is.

God has never done anything wrong. He gives people a second chance, and then a third and fourth one, too. He is kind, caring, and gentle. At the same time he is strong, mighty, powerful, knowledgeable, and wise. The better you know God, the more you love him!

God is declared *holy* in the Bible. It is a way of referring to

---

48 Revelation 17:14, 19:16
49 1 Chronicles 22:7-10
50 Matthew 18:10-14

God's incredible *greatness* and his perfect *purity*. God is *awesome*, and for our benefit, he told us about himself all through the Bible.

23 Who You Are: Your Greatness

Consider the great people of the Old Testament: Abraham, Moses, Elijah, Isaiah—and others. The God of those people is the same God that chose you to sit with him on his heavenly throne.[51] Perhaps God had a momentary lapse in judgment? No, he did not. We are so used to looking at ourselves through the world's lenses and comparing ourselves with others[52] that we sometimes forget that our vision is impaired because of fallenness.[53]

The result is that it is much easier for us to see our fallen selves—our *old man*—more clearly than our *new man*.[54] This is not unexpected, but we are called to see ourselves differently, trusting what God says about us more than what we perceive of ourselves. This should not be surprising since salvation does not alter our bodily appearance—the part of us that we can see. Rath-

---

[51] Ephesians 2:6, Revelation 3:21
[52] Romans 2:1-2, 1 Corinthians 4:3-5
[53] 2 Corinthians 3:13-18
[54] 2 Corinthians 5:16-17

er it alters a part of us that is invisible. Knowing who we are in Christ is a process that is *entirely* dependent upon learning what God says about us and his revelation of who we are by the Holy Spirit. You may expect that as a new creation how you feel and what your behavior is would be radically different, but that transformation is a part of a process that we must fight for.

Our *old man* was an entirely fallen and corrupt person, spiritually, but our old man is gone[55]. Our new man, however, exists only in a form of unity with Jesus Christ.[56] Our new selves have a divine nature that we may learn about and choose to appropriate or not.[57]

Can you imagine how priceless you are now that God is a part of your nature?

It is written: *I tell you the truth: Among those born of women there has not risen anyone greater than John the Baptist; yet he who is least in the kingdom of heaven is greater than he (*Matthew 11:11, NIV*).*

While the great people of the Old Testament may have had great accomplishments, when they walked the earth they did not have a divine nature like the least of all present-day Christians do. Be wary of thinking little of yourself, for when you do, you diminish the greatness of John the Baptist—and Abraham, Moses, Elijah, and others.

---

55 2 Corinthians 5:17
56 1 Corinthians 6:17, 19
57 2 Peter 1:4

24 Glorious Submission

Do the words *submission* or *obedience* make you cringe? They are frightening words to many people. It is no wonder—we live in a world where we have all been hurt by authority figures. There are no examples on earth of people (or governments) who have the wisdom or skill to handle their authority perfectly.

Yet God calls us to submit not only to him[58], but other people[59], and our government[60], as well. he has very good reasons. One day Jesus will be present on earth to establish his kingdom, ruling with perfect wisdom, justice, and skill. Until then, his kingdom is being established a little bit at a time by us[61]—if we are obedient to God.

It is wonderful when our desires and God's desires are the same. But we can see something more clearly by considering when

---

58 James 4:7
59 Ephesians 5:21, Hebrews 13:17
60 Romans 13:1-7, 1 Peter 2:13-15
61 Luke 22:27-30

God's will for us differs from our will. Who's kingdom are you establishing when you follow your own desires (contrary to God's will)? But if you follow God's will—in this case obeying God and those he has given authority—his kingdom is established a little more. His rightful reign is a little more fulfilled. The kingdom of light advances and the kingdom of darkness recedes.

If that was not reason enough to be obedient to God—along with the promised vast, eternal reward for obedience—submission means God, who loves you more than his own life, has more of your life covered. Obedience to God does not just mean yielding control of your life to him. It also means yielding *responsibility* for your life to him. The more you are obedient to God, the more of God's protection you receive. Read Psalm 91 and pay particular attention to the first half of verses 1 and 9.

25 Free Will vs. Predestination

There are quite a number of passages in the Bible that indicate that God has decided beforehand that certain events should take place. There are also many passages that make it clear that a person has a choice and may exercise his free will.

A conflict can arise in a person's mind when he realizes that some events fall into *both* categories—that is, a person has the free will to make a decision for which God has already decided the outcome. A good example is for a person's salvation.

Ephesians 1:5 and 1:11 both tell us that God has predetermined who will be saved. These people are called *the elect* in other places in the Bible. Romans 10:9-10 also shows us that only the people who decide to confess with their mouth that *Jesus is Lord* are saved.[62]

---

62 This passage taken in the context of the whole of Scripture refers to people that believe in Jesus, have accepted him as their lord, and have responded with action. i.e., It is no more difficult for a mute person to be saved than a person that can speak.

Many people's sense of logic tells them that *either* God has determined who will be saved *or* the person making or not making the decision for Christ has determined if he will be saved. However, this is the wrong starting point if one wants to understand these kinds of passages. Following this train of thought will lead to erroneous conclusions. A common, erroneous chain of logic that can result is: *Since God has decided already if I will be saved or not, my decision to follow or not follow Christ does not matter.*

The right starting point is to accept the fact that the Bible teaches that both are true at the same time. A person's decision to allow Jesus to be their lord or not works in conjunction with God's prior decision to save that person or not. We have free will and God will never ever act in such a way as to diminish that. God does not hold a person responsible for things that he never had control of—and we will certainly be held responsible for choosing whether Jesus is our lord or not.

In actual fact, we are always responsible for our decisions and actions, whether or not we know something of the future in advance from God or not. The fact that God has planned everything in advance does not alter that. When we read in Scripture that God has decided beforehand what will come to pass, we are getting a small glimpse into the way that God perceives everything from his sovereign perspective, but what we do with our free will is still vitally important.

26 Magic and Harry Potter

If I were to tell you that the Bible clearly portrays witchcraft[63] as something that really exists[64], would you trust that the Bible is correct? It should be no surprise that the Bible reveals the supernatural as very real, since it is first and foremost, a revelation of God himself—a supernatural being.[65]

Witchcraft, as described in the Bible, is acting on faith in supernatural forces apart from God's will. A fundamental truth every Christian needs to know about the supernatural is that our involvement in it should always be the result of *trusting God*. Praying to God is a great example—it is a powerfully supernatural act that leaves results to God[66]

Any involvement in the supernatural that does not find its

---

63 Variations are known as *witchcraft, sorcery, and divination* in the Bible
64 Pharaoh's magicians in Exodus 8 and 9, Deuteronomy 18:10-14, 1 Samuel 28, Micah 5:12. *See also* Revelation 21:8, 22:15.
65 John 4:24
66 James 5:16

roots in God's will (e.g., our own will) can be termed *witchcraft*. Another form of witchcraft occurs when our attempts to influence another person become manipulative or controlling instead of trusting God with matters outside our designated authority.

Remember the sin that caused Satan's fall? It was the *pride* of Satan when he ceased to trust God to be god, and wanted to become like God himself. The sin of pride is also *idolatry*. Idolatry is a sin that we commit whenever we trust something or someone when we should be trusting God instead. All sin can be described as a form of idolatry—it occurs when we reject God's way and instead choose to follow our way, in effect, placing ourselves above God. Exerting our will, contrary to God's will, taps into the power of Satan, even if it does not seem that way. It grants Satan a measure of involvement in what we are doing, which is *always* bad in the long term for everyone involved, just as trusting God is *always* good in the long term for everyone involved.

There is no such thing as *white* magic or *good* magic, because all magic is idolatrous in our attempt to have our way through the supernatural.

God gave us imaginations, and a child's imagination is precious indeed. It is a part of our creative nature. But is it healthy to imagine and dwell upon anything? How about visualizing and replaying murder over and over in one's mind? The difficulty in understanding why the Harry Potter stories are harmful comes from not accepting that witchcraft is real and that it is sinful and harmful. If one accepts these, then it follows that imagining sinful activities falls into the category of things we should be resisting, not nurturing.[67]

---

67 Romans 13:14, 2 Corinthians 10:4-5, Philippians 4:8, Hebrews 4:12, et al.

At the time of this writing there are five Harry Potter movies. (The author has seen the Harry Potter movies, but not read the books.) The movies become progressively dark. Not only do they become darker in mood, but also in their display of witchcraft and rebellion. As the movies progress, more powerful forms of witchcraft are used to resolve conflicts. Rebellion by the children is sometimes rewarded by the authorities. The people become more intense and violent in their efforts to be controlling. The lowest point is when a death is graphically portrayed due to witchcraft, and in response, the supposed good guy, Harry Potter, uses illegal magic to torture someone.

No doubt some of the appeal of the Harry Potter stories is seeing Harry able to fight back in otherwise impossible situations. During our lives we are all faced with painful choices. Often the best moral choice is more painful than the alternatives. Sometimes this leaves us feeling helpless, especially when the most painful choice is to do nothing. Demonstrating witchcraft as a resolution to painful situations sets a terrible example, since at the low points of our lives when we are searching for any way out of our pain (a situation used by God for us to turn to him for help), a person may instead turn to witchcraft, even when its reality is questioned.

When we see our role models (or anyone) do something, it opens a door for us to imitate the same behavior. The effects of *desensitization* cannot be understated. The Harry Potter stories desensitize us to witchcraft as well as the *idea* of witchcraft. Children and adults consequently find it easier to explore self-directed supernatural solutions rather than turning to God for the help we need in our lives—with guaranteed terrible long term consequences.

For the Christian who feels led to investigate witchcraft as described in the Bible further may find two good resources to be Neil T. Anderson's *The Bondage Breaker* (Eugene: Harvest House Publishers, 1993) and Rick Joyner's *Overcoming Witchcraft* (Charlotte: MorningStar Publications, 2001).

27 In the Name of Jesus Christ

Christians end their prayers with it. Christians certainly end their commands to spirits with it. But *what is it?*

My understanding of what *in the name of Jesus Christ* means came from several Bible passages, none of which contain one of the several promises that God will give us whatever we ask for in Jesus' name.[68]

A close examination of both Matthew 8:5-13 and Luke 7:1-10 reveals both passages are about the same event during Jesus' ministry. The alert reader will notice that these two passages have an apparent contradiction: In the Matthew passage the Centurion comes himself to Jesus to ask that his sick servant be healed. In the Luke passage, the Centurion sends elders in his place.

The resolution of this apparent contradiction yields a pearl of insight that is consistent with other passages of Scripture—usually about fathers and sons. The Centurion sent someone in his

---

68   John 14:13-14, John 15:16, John 23-24, 26

place with his authority and his words, and everyone treated the messenger as if he were equal to the Centurion to such a degree that Matthew considered it acceptable to just say the Centurion came himself.

The tight relationship between the one in authority and the one he has sent can be seen in John 12:44-45 (NIV), *Then Jesus cried out, "When a man believes in me, he does not believe in me only, but in the one who sent me. When he looks at me, he sees the one who sent me.*

It can also be seen in John 5:17-47. In John 5:17-19 (NIV) Jesus says, ..."*My Father is always at his work to this very day, and I, too, am working."* ... *he was even calling God his own Father, making himself equal with God. Jesus gave them this answer: "I tell you the truth, the Son can do nothing by himself; he can do only what he sees his Father doing, because whatever the Father does the Son also does.*

Then in John 5:30 (NIV), Jesus says, *By myself I can do nothing; I judge only as I hear, and my judgment is just, for I seek not to please myself but him who sent me.*

And then in John 5:43 (NIV), Jesus says (bold added), ***I have come in my Father's name***, *and you do not accept me; but if someone else comes in his own name, you will accept him.*

Jesus describes his coming as *in his Father's name*. It is most appropriate for us to say *in Jesus name* or *in the name of Jesus Christ* when we are intending to proclaim the fact that we are working within the will of Jesus Christ, and are walking in the authority that Jesus has granted us for his work.

While God has many standing commands for us in which we may confidently affirm we are being obedient with *in Jesus name*, it is clear that knowing God's will for us for the moment allows us to walk consistently and continually with his authority.

Romans 12:1-2 (NIV, bold added) helps us know how to get there: *Therefore, I urge you, brothers, in view of God's mercy, to offer your bodies as living sacrifices, holy and pleasing to God— this is your spiritual act of worship. Do not conform any longer to the pattern of this world, but be transformed by the renewing of your mind.* ***Then you will be able to test and approve what God's will is—his good, pleasing and perfect will.***

28   Wealth and Claiming Verses

See also *God: Person Or Machine?*

There is a practice that is sometimes called Name It And Claim It. Name It And Claim It is also done by people without thinking of it by that name. It happens when a Christian believes that the Bible is the inerrant Word of God, but she comes across a promise of God that she is not yet experiencing. She wants to receive the benefits of the promise, and so proclaims her faith in God by naming the promise and stating that she claims it for herself. The purpose of naming it and claiming it in the person's mind may be that it is a part of the process that is needed to experience the promise. In some cases, people use this approach to claim financial prosperity, i.e., wealth.

As an expression of faith, there is not necessarily anything wrong with this. We are children of God and if this is how someone wishes to express their trust in God, it surely pleases God.

However, questions eventually arise if the person does not seem to be receiving what God promises after some time.

God's promises to us in the Bible are there for several reasons. One is so that we may know God better. God promises to keep our consciousness alive in spite of bodily death. Reading that and also that he will take us to his presence where we will never again experience fear or suffering tells us something about God's character. It also gives us hope. Hope is very much needed in this life. It is the source of a great amount of our will and power to live, and God gives it generously.

Another reason God put promises in the Bible is so that we may experience him in our lives. Peter gives us a rich passage in 1 Peter 1:3-5 (NIV): *His divine power has given us everything we need for life and godliness through our knowledge of him who called us by his own glory and goodness. Through these he has given us his very great and precious promises, so that through them you may participate in the divine nature and escape the corruption in the world caused by evil desires. For this very reason, make every effort to add to your faith goodness ...*

Peter is not referring to escaping the corruption in the world when we die, but while we are still alive. He is telling us that what we need for life and godliness is a knowledge of God. He also says that the escape from corruption is by participating in God's nature—and that comes through God's promises. As Peter begins verse 5 he implies these come through a foundation of faith. Name It And Claim It has powerful truths at its core. However, an error often occurs in understanding what our role is to receive the effects of God's promises.

Our faith in God is not a simple thing. It is complex and has many facets. It is the life-giving, life-maintaining, power-wielding invisible substance of our relationship with God. It is the substance through which God transforms our character, our lives, and the world. We do not receive God's promises by proclaiming that we claim them. We receive them by knowing and trusting God, which **only comes through the sanctification and faith that God grants**.[69]

A good, general purpose test of valid spiritual power and its blessings is this: ask yourself if it is from you or from God. Claiming a promise of God depends on me doing the claiming. (See *Magic and Harry Potter*.) In the end you get the power of whatever comes from doing the claiming, which is absolutely nothing.

Another test is to ask yourself, who is deciding when it will happen. If you are claiming a promise that you want to receive now or even sometime in the near future, it is you that is trying to control the timing of something that only God can do.

Instead, the God-prescribed method to receive God's promises is to ask God and keep asking![70] If you would like to also ask God for the faith to believe in his promise, go ahead. Believing can be very empowering and can dispel hopelessness and despair.

God often wants to accomplish many things for you along the way to the experienced promise. Ask him to show you why you aren't experiencing the promise yet. Also ask him to keep you moving forward in your walk with him. Our job is usually just to abide in Christ.[71] All of God's promises will eventually come to those who are patient.

See also *What Is Faith, Really?*

---

69 Ephesians 2:8
70 Matthew 7:7-11, Luke 11:5-13
71 John 15:4-7

29   The Real Satan

Originally, Satan[72] was called Lucifer or *morning star* (both mean *light-bearer*) and he was one of God's angels—a spiritual being. God created him good, along with the other angels, our universe, and man. Having free will, the angels had to choose to follow God, just as we do with our free will. However, unlike us, the angels lived constantly in God's presence.[73]

Lucifer's original sin was that of extreme arrogance (Biblical *pride*). He saw what it was like to be God and he aspired to be God—he was not content to acknowledge God as the only god. When his desire became his intention, he sinned and was thrown out of heaven along with the angels who had chosen to follow him. His name became *Satan* (which means *adversary*) and his angels were then called demons, evil spirits, and sometimes devils.

Having sinned while being fully in God's presence, Satan committed the ultimate crime—a crime that humans cannot commit since we do not have such a full knowledge of God and his

---
72   Isaiah 14:12-14, Ezekiel 28:11-19
73   Matthew 18:10

love as Lucifer did. The effect of his crime was that his nature fell into complete, irredeemable corruption. Satan became fully evil and lost the ability to choose to do good. He only knows evil and can only do evil—his intentions are always to deceive, steal, murder, and destroy.[74] His foremost agenda is to keep people separated from God, God's love, and God's salvation.

Consider the most evil people in human history—the people filled with such hate or fear that they torture people, commit mass murder, or attempt genocide. The worst of them are imitations of Satan. When considering Satan, envision *concentration camps* instead of horns, a red suit, or a respectful, elegant evil being as he is often portrayed in movies.

Some people are concerned about God's power vs. Satan's power. The war they (and we) fight is not a war of power, but of human wills. God has infinite power and Satan has finite power. Near the end of the war, God will send just one angel to chain Satan against his will and cast him down.[75]

---

74 John 8:44, John 10:10
75 Revelation 20:1-3

30 Can Satan Read My Mind?

See also *The Real Satan*.

It is a huge mistake to think you are protected from Satan (and his demonic servants) because he is a limited, created being. That idea, if accepted and integrated into your thinking about other spiritual matters, will result in all manner of error.

For example, while it is generally accepted, and the author agrees, that Satan is not omnipresent, the verses that are usually used to make that point[76] do not give 100% assurance that he is not. After all, God, who is omnipresent, is shown as traveling through the garden of Eden.[77]

The starting point for understanding Satan's power is Jude 1:9 (NIV): But even the archangel Michael, when he was disputing with the devil about the body of Moses, did not dare to bring

---

76   Job 1:7, 2:2
77   Genesis 3:8

a slanderous accusation against him, but said, "The Lord rebuke you!"

This is the only place in the Bible that an angel is named an archangel—a chief angel (although there is at least one other[78]). It stands to reason that God, through Jude, is trying to make a point. Even a chief angel did not dare to incite Satan.

If you examine the many encounters humans have with angels in the Bible, you will understand that there really is no comparison in power between a fleshly human and any angel. It is not unusual for a person to be overcome by simply being in the presence of an angel.

An angel can roll a heavy stone away from a grave door[79]—why not demons? Satan can masquerade as an angel[80]—would he really do this if it were not effective? Angels can appear in our dreams[81]—why not Satan or his lesser servants, as well?

You may just be finding out that Satan may be more capable and powerful than you thought, but that does not impart any new ability to him than he already had.

The real issue is not whether or not Satan can read our minds, but that our only real protection from Satan and demons comes solely from God. God grants a great degree of protection to both Christians and non-Christians. He has many blessings for non-Christians as well as Christians.[82] He loves us all, and fortunately for us, he is infinitely more powerful and capable than Satan is.

However, do not rest in the protection you have always had. Your power against the darkness can grow. Your power is found

---

78 Daniel 10:13
79 Matthew 28:2
80 2 Corinthians 11:14-15
81 Matthew 1:20, 2:13, 19
82 Matthew 5:45

in understanding and believing the truth about God—who he is and who you are to him.

See also *Who Is God?*

31 The Slipperiest Deceptions

Are you aware of any of Satan's schemes against Christians? The apostle Paul pointed out that one of Satan's schemes is to keep us from forgiving and comforting a brother (or sister) in Christ who had completed a time of punishment.[83]

There are hosts of schemes that Satan has against various Christians. If you examine almost any Biblical passage, you can guess at a scheme—they all have one thing in common: they are meant to steer you away from God and Jesus Christ.

The slipperiest deceptions are the ones that hide themselves well. What if a Christian believes that he is a good follower of Christ, when in fact, he is not?[84] Or perhaps, believes he is saved because his church told him he is, when in fact, he is not? Then he will not be looking for a way to correct his condition, and will feel anyone that points his problem out to him is in error. He may

---
83 2 Corinthians 2:11
84 Matthew 7:21-23

The Slipperiest Deceptions

reject the very capable and competent people that God sends to help him. We must learn to listen for God's voice in everything. God can and will speak to us even through non-Christians and non-living things.

Some of the slipperiest deceptions occur when Satan gets you to **believe in spiritual truths in the wrong way**. This scheme can be powerful, because it may appear that you have a new insight, which is something that God *does* grant as we learn from him. (See also *Christian Cults and Cliques*.) This often happens when new Christians are trying to understand God's requirement to be obedient to him along with his grace for us to be ourselves.

Another way it happens when we elevate any spiritual truth to a place that only God himself should occupy. Oftentimes this will appear as something *you* must do or not do in a circumstance when the proper perspective would result in just trusting God.

For example, do you believe that through knowing, understanding, and believing the Bible, you are better protected from Satan? While this is true in an indirect sense, if you focus on the Bible's words for your protection, you may miss the fact that your protection comes only from God himself.

Regarding salvation, oftentimes deceptions lead us to beliefs where we may say that if *I* do or do not do something, ... when in fact your eternal security *depends on God alone through Jesus Christ*. We can ascribe power to something other than God for our security, but it is only from God himself that we receive anything good.[85] Can you see why having faith in God is essential to our well-being? We must learn to accept God's love and help for us. We can do nothing on our own![86] All the obedience, Bible study,

---
85 James 1:17
86 John 5:30, 8:28, 15:5

church attendance, repentance of sins, and even faith and love in the world can not replace God himself in our lives.

If you are supremely blessed to truly believe that the God of the Bible and his Son, Jesus Christ, are alive and well today in heaven, and are working on earth for the deliverance and salvation of many[87], and it is your desire to be obedient and pleasing to your heavenly Father with your words, actions, and activities, then you can rest from all worry about your spiritual condition. Your heart is in the best possible place, fully pleasing to God. He will help you however you need help. All you need to do is *keep moving forward* when you can, and just *stand*[88] and *remain in Christ*[89] during difficult times. He is your real protection against the slipperiest deceptions.

---

[87] See Luke 4:18-19 for one of Jesus' messages about why he came.
[88] Ephesians 6:11, 13, 14
[89] John 15:4-5, 7, 9-10 (*abide* in the NASB)

32 Christian Cults and Cliques

Words like *fundamentalist* and *radical* have negative connotations to many people, even though the simplest definitions for them are not sinister. The associations that spring to mind for the word *cult* are even worse. *Cult* is usually the word of choice when describing an apparently religious group of people involved in mass suicides or deviant social behavior. Christian theologians often have a specific definition of what constitutes a cult. (There is no attempt to define it in this chapter.) However, a group of people need not have those extreme symptoms to still be following cult-like, spiritually dangerous beliefs.

It is every Christian's responsibility to become familiar enough with the Bible so that the seeds of cultism can be dealt with in their own hearts when they arise. When the seeds of cultism are small enough, they are just the normal errors that we all make as we learn the Bible and get to know God better. We are all imperfect people prone to drawing wrong conclusions when we do not understand a matter as thoroughly as we could.

The most spiritually dangerous thing any of us can do is give a place to someone or something in our lives that only God himself should occupy. It is the sin of idolatry and happens when we trust some object or person instead of God. We *all* have done this in a variety of ways, the most common being when we put our trust in our own judgment rather than God's judgment. It also occurs when we trust a leader of the church, or any other person, instead of trusting God. While it is a subtle distinction, it also happens when we trust God's words instead of trusting God himself.

It is important that we understand who our teacher is. It is not our pastor, or the person in our Bible study group that explains Bible passages, or a book author. Jesus says in John 16:13 (NIV), *...when he, the Spirit of truth, comes, he will guide you into all truth....* In Matthew 23:8-10 (NIV) Jesus also says, *"But you are not to be called 'Rabbi,' for you have only one Master and you are all brothers. And do not call anyone on earth 'father,' for you have one Father, and he is in heaven. Nor are you to be called 'teacher,' for you have one Teacher, the Christ."* Jesus is not telling his disciples not to call their dads *father*; he is teaching them about not letting anyone take God's place in their lives.

Regarding prophecies, the apostle Paul wrote in 1 Thessalonians 5:21-22 (NIV), *Test everything. Hold on to the good. Avoid every kind of evil.* Prophecies are one kind of message from God. God's command, through Paul, is appropriately applied to any teaching that is said to be from God. It tells us that sometimes what we hear will be a mix of truths and lies, and that we need to take the truths to heart, but reject the lies.

Regarding sharing a common yoke and having similar lives

to non-Christians, God tells us in 2 Corinthians 6:17-18 (NIV), *"Therefore come out from them and be separate, says the Lord. Touch no unclean thing, and I will receive you. I will be a Father to you, and you will be my sons and daughters, says the Lord Almighty."* This is a strong passage and is one of the passages that explains why devoted followers of Christ should neither marry nor form tightly bound business partnerships with non-Christians. But it can be misunderstood—as well as understood, but carried too far. It does not mean we should move to the mountains or avoid contact with non-Christians. It is a seed of cultism when a passage like this is used to motivate Christians to *elitism*.

Elitism is an attitude that can occur when one believes he belongs to a select group of individuals—a group of people that is *more special* than other people. For Christians, it may be a group of people that believes they are a part of God's inner circle, or have a special calling that is more important than the normal calls God puts on people's lives. There even may be deceptive *false humility* about it, such as when this person or group of people is willing to suffer for their "higher calling."

One terrible form of exalting themselves is when a group of Christians comes to believe they are God's servants for judgment—in punishing people for their sins or even inappropriately telling people about their sins. (Have they been granted that role by their hearers?)

The *come out from them* passage is balanced by another message from Paul in 1 Corinthians 9:19-22, where he says he makes himself a slave to everyone so that they might be saved. He becomes like a Jew for the sake of the Jews (but never sinning), because that enables Jews to accept and relate to him sufficiently that they will hear what Paul wants to tell them about Jesus. There is great importance in this example from Paul. It tells us that behaving in extremely odd ways as compared to the people that see our behavior as followers of Jesus is not usually what God wants. The sinners of Jesus' time found His company enjoyable, undoubtedly due in part to his generous and gracious attitude about their sin, instead of the condemning one they were used to hearing from the religious leaders.

Another form of Christian elitism happens when a group of people within a local church start seeing themselves as having superior insight into something of God's compared to the rest of the church. It can happen with elders as well as with prayer groups. It can happen with pro-charismatic Christians or anti-charismatic Christians, or even a group of people that disapproves of the worship music. The picture that Paul gives us of the *body* of Christ in 1 Corinthians 12 is a picture of how church members are related that **almost painfully maintains equality between the members of the body.** Scripture makes it plain that God does not show favoritism.[90] All Christians are his children and all are equally special to him.

Lastly, while it is spiritually dangerous to find yourself listening to the teaching of cultic church leaders, it is also spiritually dangerous for Christians without a good foundation of Biblical knowledge *not* to rely on their church leadership. Church elders are a vital component of a healthy church. Given the opportunity, they will keep church members from straying too far into false doctrine. Whenever you find yourself not knowing who to believe, the answer is always God. Ask God for help. If your heart is in the right place, God will reveal the truth to you, act on your behalf, or lead you to where you need to be. Being involved in

---

90 Acts 10:34, Romans 2:11, Ephesians 6:9, Colossians 3:25, James 2:9

the process of becoming familiar enough with the Bible that you know how to look up answers to questions you have is a priceless skill that you will use over and over. It will take less time than you think if you commit to regular Bible study with capable leaders.

33 Jesus, The Fulfillment of the Law

Matthew 5:17 (NIV, text in brackets added): *Do not think that I* [Jesus] *have come to abolish the Law or the Prophets; I have not come to abolish them but to fulfill them.*

Jesus makes this statement in Matthew 5:17 and then goes on to explain how the Law will exist until heaven and earth pass away. Nowhere in the Bible is there a single passage that explains all of what it means that Jesus came to fulfill the Law. Pieces of it are in different places. The part of the verse that refers to Jesus fulfilling the Prophets refers to the many prophecies that the Old Testament prophets made about God's coming savior. Jesus came and fulfilled all of these prophecies.

Fulfilling the Law is a reference to several things. One is the fact that the Law required a sacrifice to be made to pay for sins, and that Jesus did what the Law required to pay for our sins (made a sacrifice of himself).

Believing in and trusting God forms a very real spiritual connection with God. So Jesus fulfilling the Law is also a reference to the fact that we actually share in Jesus' death (and resurrection) through faith in him. It is correct to say that in a spiritual way we also died on the cross with Jesus (so our sins are no more), and we have been raised into new life with the resurrection of Jesus.

Also, since Jesus kept the whole Law while he was on earth, we have, through faith in Jesus, kept the whole Law as well.

Jesus came to earth precisely so he could die to pay for our sins and to be raised into new life so that we might partake of the payment for sins and resurrection to new life.

These are spiritual realities, not symbolism. (See also Cycle of the Spirit.) These spiritual truths have an outworking in the physical realm: We must physically die, because that completes the death that we died with Jesus and eliminates the sinful nature that remains with us in the physical realm. When we are physically raised into our new body given by God, that will complete the resurrection we already share with Jesus in spirit.

A natural question is why can someone else can pay for my sins? After all, God said in Ezekiel 18:20 (NIV), *The soul who sins is the one who will die. The son will not share the guilt of the father, nor will the father share the guilt of the son. The righteousness of the righteous man will be credited to him, and the wickedness of the wicked will be charged against him.*

The answer to this question is found in different parts of the Law. Since the Law is an expression of God's nature, and not a set of arbitrary rules, it is something that God revealed about himself. The most commonly understood way Jesus fulfilled the law was in his role as our high priest.

Much of the book of Hebrews describes Jesus in this role. Our need for a high priest is summarized in Hebrews 2:17 (NIV): *For this reason he had to be made like his brothers in every way, in order that he might become a merciful and faithful high priest in service to God, and that he might make atonement for the sins of the people.*

Jesus' service as our high priest fulfilled the requirements in the Law for paying for the sins of the high priest's people. Not only that, in his high priestly role, after Jesus died, his job was not quite finished. As our high priest he needed to present the sacrifice (himself) to God in the most holy place of the heavenly tabernacle. We see that he did just that in Hebrews 9:11-12 and 23-26.

Another way Jesus fulfilled the Law is referred to as Jesus' kinsman-redeemer role for us. The main passage describes how a relative can be purchased back out of slavery.

Leviticus 25:47-49 (NIV, bold added): *If an alien or a temporary resident among you becomes rich and one of your countrymen becomes poor and* **sells himself to the alien living among you** *or to a member of the alien's clan, he retains the right of redemption after he has sold himself. One of his relatives may redeem him: An uncle or a cousin or* **any blood relative in his clan may redeem him.** ...

Although we are not slaves to other people, Jesus teaches us a new way to view our sin problem in John 8:34 (NIV): *Jesus replied, I tell you the truth, everyone who sins is a slave to sin.* It is appropriate to consider slavery to sin to also mean slavery to Satan.

Paul references the fact that by sinning we have sold ourselves as slaves in Romans 7:14 (NIV, bold added): *We know that the law is spiritual; but I am unspiritual,* **sold as a slave to sin.**

Our need then was for a blood relative to purchase us back

from slavery to sin—someone who was able to pay the price. Another slave is not able to pay the price since all that he is and owns belongs to his master. We needed someone that was not a slave to sin to purchase us. Fortunately, there was one such person, Jesus Christ, who was sinless in every way.[91]

He became a blood relative (Hebrews 2:14-15, NIV): *Since the children have flesh and blood, he too shared in their humanity so that by his death he might destroy him who holds the power of death—that is, the devil—and free those who all their lives were held in slavery by their fear of death.*

The price that needed to be paid to free us from our slavery to sin was very high. We had incurred a debt of death according to the Law,[92] so as our kinsman-redeemer, Jesus, had to die to pay this debt so we would be freed from slavery to sin—and so, because of his great love for us, that is exactly what he chose to do.

The short book of Ruth gives us a wonderful picture of Boaz being a kinsman-redeemer for Ruth.

---

91   Hebrews 4:15
92   from being obedient to sin, an example of intentional sin. (See also Romans 6:23)

34 Did God Really Command the Israelites to Kill Children and Infants?

This is what the LORD Almighty says: I will punish the Amalekites for what they did to Israel when they waylaid them as they came up from Egypt. Now go, attack the Amalekites and totally destroy everything that belongs to them. Do not spare them; put to death men and women, children and infants, cattle and sheep, camels and donkeys. (1 Samuel 15:2-3, NIV)

This is one of the most difficult passages in the Bible for some people to accept. It is so difficult that even Christians who believe the Bible is all true can waffle when pressed on what this passage means. All manner of conjecture springs to mind in an effort to resolve this in a way that seems to make sense.

It is not actually the passage that is hard to understand,

though. The passage is not complicated, but what it does is drive us to question our understanding of who God is. Accepting that our loving God did this is what is difficult.

The news and entertainment of our time exposes us to an ever increasing amount of both real and imaginary violence. No one can take it all in without being desensitized. Our desensitization is a defense mechanism by design. Otherwise, our appropriate responses of sadness, pain, and grief would be overwhelming for the amount of bad news we see, hear, read about, and experience. An effect of this defense mechanism is to "get used" to a certain amount of evil. Another effect is that we develop the attitude that pain is bad, because that is what our entire being is telling us when we experience it.

But pain is amoral—it is neither morally good nor evil. A vaccine against a devastating disease given by injection can be considered good by every moral measure, except it may also be painful. We do not accuse a physician for doing something bad when she administers the injection properly, but it still may nevertheless hurt.

Our desensitization to evil has diminished some of our sensitivity for the need for justice and its associated punishments. That is one of the reasons it is difficult for many to accept God's orders to commit genocide against the Amalekites.

Not all of us are numbed to the need for justice, however. If you are someone to whom a great injustice has been done—the sudden, violent death of someone you love, for example—you probably have retained a sense for the need for justice. Many of the Psalms express David's anguish at God's supposed delay in bringing justice against his enemies. We have the right to desire justice be done. This is an aspect of the character of God.

God did not give a choice to Saul or the Israelites to kill all the Amalekites. It is God who was responsible for the punishment of the Amalekites, not the Israelites. This is important to understand, because it was punishment. It was the result of God passing judgment, something the Israelites did not have the authority to do.

Another reason accepting this passage is difficult is because the destruction is described so vividly. Consider this: God will condemn billions of people to hell on judgment day.[93] This is (perhaps) an easier thought to have, because it is less vivid, but it is nonetheless a much more terrible event than the death of the Amalekites.

This passage also challenges us because a part of us recognizes that what God commanded is so extremely severe that it makes us uneasy. After all, while we may not have committed the sins the Amalekites did, we still commit sins. This passage paints a terrible picture of what our subconscious might think could happen to us. This is a remnant of our old thinking, however.

There is actually no reason to fear anything for the child of God. Pain and suffering in this life, if you can accept it, is not something to be feared. It is our goal to trust God in the midst of pain (and please leave it to God to make it happen). As God matures us in this particular way, pain loses its power over us. Finally, after this life, there will never again be pain or suffering for the children of God.[94]

Lastly, why did God condemn the Amalekite children and infants to death? I do not know. But I do know this: every human born inherits a sin nature[95] and thereby deserves an eternity in hell. It is a hard truth that we need God's grace, but it is true. It

---
93   Matthew 7:13-14
94   Revelation 21:4
95   Romans 3:23

is very easy to become accustomed to God's mercy, because he is so incredibly and frequently merciful. He showed mercy to the Amorites for centuries before passing judgment.[96] But he has not done anything wrong if he withholds it. And while I would not use it as my source of comfort, it is possible that God saved the Amalekite infants and youngest children eternally.[97] (It is more appropriate to find your comfort in the grace that God has extended to you and his reliably loving nature.)

Look for God's mercy along with his justice in Ezekiel 18:21-32.

---

96   Genesis 15:16
97   2 Samuel 12:23

35 Pointing A Gun

God is ultimately responsible for the fact that we are alive. It is he that sustains our life until such time as he decides otherwise.[98] No one on earth has the right to murder another person—but it is still done. A murderer must violate someone's God-given right to life to kill them.

But the murderer does not become a murderer when his victim dies. He becomes a murderer when his thought to murder turns into an intention.[99] God knows when a thought turns into an intention, but we cannot. Our governmental laws reflect our inability to see a person's intentions. The laws examine only the verifiable physical world facts—primarily what a person's actions were.

Accommodating that limitation means that at the moment a person points a gun at another with the intention or possible intention to murder, he yields his right to life. Both God's justice and our laws allow that the offender can be killed if it will stop the crime from being committed. A police officer who kills the gun

---
98   John 21:22, Acts 5:1-11
99   Matthew 5:21-22

pointer has done a good thing—not the taking of the life which is always sad—but of preventing someone from destroying the only life the potential victim has.

The issue of capital punishment is regularly brought into the light of public debate. Often the focus is its deterrent effect, which is an important aspect of what a just sentence is, because crimes affect a whole community, through the friends and relatives of the criminal and the victim, and even of those who simply read about the crime.

However, the primary focus should be on what a just *punishment* is. Our own fear of death gives many of us queasiness about capital punishment. None of us wants to experience capital punishment, and we project our fear onto the criminal and say it should not be done to him, either.

Just punishment has its foundation in believing in and knowing a God of justice. Our increasingly secular society has no choice but to look to other sources such as its deterrent effect and what "seems right." That capital punishment leaves no room for remediation of the criminal is seen as an argument against capital punishment. The misunderstanding in that is punishment is often seen as a mode of *correction*. While they both have their place, just punishment need not be corrective.

The death penalty is a more severe form of *punishment* than decades in prison, but it is not *cruel* or *unusual* punishment, and allowing a criminal to live can sometimes be the greatest injustice of all.

(This chapter does not address coping with flaws in the justice system.)

36 Euthanasia and Suicide

There are some issues that God does not tell us how to handle, but tells us not to handle them. The example often used is for *vengeance*. Romans 12:19 (NIV) says *Do not take revenge, my friends, but leave room for God's wrath, for it is written: "It is mine to avenge; I will repay," says the Lord.*[100]

God also addresses sexual immorality this way in 1 Corinthians 6:18 (NIV) *Flee from sexual immorality...*

God's commands are solely for our benefit. He himself profits not at all by giving us commands and wisdom to live by, except the opportunity for a better relationship with us. If anything could be said to be for his advantage, it would be that he wants to bless us with eternal blessings and obeying his commands give him just cause—but he still blesses us even without just cause.

The foremost passage that must be dealt with on the subject of euthanasia and suicide is 1 Corinthians 3:16-17 (NIV): *Don't you*

---
100   *See also* Romans 12:17-21

know that you yourselves are God's temple and that God's Spirit lives in you? If anyone destroys God's temple, God will destroy him; for God's temple is sacred, and you are that temple.[101]

It is not that this passage is difficult to understand, per se—but that it is difficult to *apply* correctly to a specific situation. There are many Biblical issues that must be understood to be able to apply it to, say, a specific instance of suicide or attempted suicide.[102] Beware of thinking you understand the passage "clearly." Consider this: God has not given us the ability to know 100% whether another person has received salvation or not, and salvation is a topic covered at length in the Bible. Wouldn't it be more difficult to discern the truths for a suicide for which very little is written in Scripture?

From 1 Corinthians 3:16-17 we can gather that the last few seconds of life of even the most "worthless" person are priceless—because there is much more to us than our physical shell. (See *Little Gods*.) To decide when a person should die is a decision of unfathomable magnitude. God has only granted this authority to the government in instances of criminal punishment.[103] None of us are given the right to decide when someone else or ourselves should die.

A person considers suicide when he or she can not see any way out of their pain. Those with moderate or severe depression are unable to be hopeful, even if there is a good reason to be. A person can be stuck in the darkest place of her soul, or live with excruciating physical pain. Such a person may pray that God would do *anything* rather than let her continue in that place. The

---

101 *See also* 1 Corinthians 6:19-20 and John 21:22
102 For example, if a suicide is the result of profound clinical depression, is it an effect of the illness, and not that person's fault?
103 Romans 13:1-4

idea of death becomes a sought after friend, not a fear, during those times. The Book of Job can be a comfort in those times. It helps us know the truth, that we are not alone in our suffering.

One cannot know anyone else's suffering. Consider that when in pain, a person does not usually even feel she understands *her own pain*. It is a place where questioning and confusion are hallmarks. It is vital to hold onto the truth that God loves you more than you can imagine and that it was never his intention that anyone should suffer. Suffering entered the world with sin. For times that seem vastly too long we all spend part of our lives in pain. Trust God that no matter what happens, He will eventually rescue you—usually in this life, but if not, at the natural end of it.

Suicide and euthanasia are sins, but learn this lesson: few things in life, as described in Scripture, fall into the categories of *always* or *never*.

(This chapter is not about people in a vegetative state.)

37 Adam's vs. Eve's Sin

1 Timothy 2:8-15 contains a famously controversial passage. Verses 11-14 (NIV) say, *A woman should learn in quietness and full submission. I do not permit a woman to teach or to have authority over a man; she must be silent. For Adam was formed first, then Eve. And Adam was not the one deceived; it was the woman who was deceived and became a sinner.*

Before the quoted passage above, verse 9 tells us that the apostle Paul's words are influenced by the culture of those times. Some people have called Paul a misogynist, but we must consider that Paul was taught by God.[104] That accusation really has no valid basis. This is the same Paul that wrote that Jews, Greeks, slaves, free people, males, and females are all one in Christ and all receive an equal share of God's inheritance as children of God,[105] an equality that was unheard of in the culture of that time.

There is a different reason Paul says what he did—in fact there are two reasons—Paul gives them in the passage itself:

---
104 Galatians 1:11-12
105 Galatians 3:28-29, Colossians 3:11

- For Adam was formed first, then Eve. (1 Timothy 2:13, NIV)
- Adam was not the one deceived; it was the woman who was deceived and became a sinner. (1 Timothy 2:14, NIV)

When you find a passage in the Bible that you don't like, stop and get your bearings. God created our world and us without sin. His immediate reaction upon finding out it had been corrupted came from his great love. Considering what the consequence could have been for breaking the only command God gave Adam and Eve, God's passed a rather mild judgment. At the same time, he made a reference to the rescue from Satan he was going to provide (through Jesus Christ)[106], as well as equipped Adam and Eve for their life in a fallen world.[107]

All of God's actions and commands are to help devoted followers of Christ over the long term.[108] If we could see the spiritual realm as we see the physical, we could develop good spiritual habits because we would be able to see the consequences of our choices. But we can't see the spiritual, so we need to listen to what God has to say to direct our lives to have good results.

The first point given in 1 Timothy 2:13 can only be a reference to something God put in Adam's and Eve's nature because Paul is appealing to the original source of male and female. To Paul's readers, being formed first would have been understood in the context of firstborn in a family, either the first child or an ancestor born before a descendant.[109] In both cases, the greatness

---
106 Genesis 3:15
107 Genesis 3:21
108 Romans 8:28
109 John 1:30, et al.

of the firstborn was greater. (See also Leadership Responsibility.) Comparative greatness between humans dictates that the elder always has at least the greatness of the younger.[110] Paul is saying that there is something in the nature of husbands that gives them a firstborn-like authority over their wives. (As is confirmed elsewhere, women should submit to their husbands,[111] but it should not be read as a plain black and white submission. It is a different kind of submission than to God. It is similar to the difference between respect for one's husband vs. reverence for God. [There are also Biblical obligations for husbands.[112]])

Please note: the greatness of someone born earlier was emphasized in that culture, but it is also a spiritual law that applies to all people in all times. Additionally, the appeal to Adam being firstborn is something that Paul would not have made if the relationship between the male and female was not otherwise equal. If Eve was more like a slave to Adam, Paul could not have made the firstborn appeal.

The second point given in 1 Timothy 2:14 is a reference by Paul to something in the nature of women that makes them more easily deceived. He is explaining the reason for his statement in verses 11-12. But he is not putting women down. Far from it, in fact. What he is saying is that women are more easily deceived and then more prone to committing unintentional sins, and men are more prone to committing intentional sins!

What an awful inheritance that men have received from Adam! Eve sinned first, but her sin was unintentional—she was deceived. Adam sinned second, but his sin was intentional. He was not deceived; he knew what he was doing. To understand the

---

110 Matthew 10:24-25, Luke 6:40, John 15:20
111 Ephesians 5:22, 25, Colossians 3:18
112 There are many, but especially note Ephesians 5:25

seriousness of this, look at this passage:

*But only the high priest entered the inner room, and that only once a year, and never without blood, which he offered for himself and for the sins the people had committed in **ignorance**.* (Hebrews 9:7, NIV, bold added)

The Law that God gave to Moses, which reflects God's nature, described what must be done for the atonement of unintentional sins.[113] But this is what God said about intentional sins:

*"'But anyone who sins defiantly, whether native-born or alien, blasphemes the LORD, and that person must be cut off from his people. Because he has despised the LORD's word and broken his commands, that person must surely be cut off; **his guilt remains on him**.'"* (Numbers 15:30-31, NIV, bold added)

There was nothing a person could do to be forgiven of intentional sins under the Law! (However, through the more perfect atonement of Jesus Christ's death, all sins, unintentional and intentional, are forgiven.[114]) Adam's sin was enormously worse than Eve's.

In spite of Paul's reasoning that took the nature of men and women into account, 1 Timothy 2:8-15 is still written to people that lived in a different culture than we have today. He is not saying that all women are more easily deceived than all men, and he is not saying that all men are better leaders than all women. God, through Paul, is referring to something in the nature of men and women to prescribe appropriate roles for each in the culture of that time so that all would benefit.

---

113   Leviticus 16, Numbers 15:22-29
114   Hebrews 10:10-22

38 Authority, Power, and Responsibility

au·thor·i·ty [*uh*-**thawr**-i-tee, *uh*-**thor**-] *–noun* 1b. the right to control, command, or determine[115]

pow·er [**pou**-er] *–noun* 1. ability to do or act; capability of doing or accomplishing something[116]

re·spon·si·bil·i·ty [ri-spon-*suh*-**bil**-i-tee] *–noun* 1. the state or fact of being responsible. 3. a particular burden of obligation upon one who is responsible: *the responsibilities of authority.*[117]

---

115   authority. Dictionary.com. *Dictionary.com Unabridged (v 1.1).* Random House, Inc. http://dictionary.reference.com/browse/authority (accessed: December 26, 2007).

116   power. Dictionary.com. *Dictionary.com Unabridged (v 1.1).* Random House, Inc. http://dictionary.reference.com/browse/power (accessed: December 26, 2007).

117   responsibility. Dictionary.com. *Dictionary.com Unabridged (v 1.1).* Random House, Inc. http://dictionary.reference.com/browse/responsibility (accessed: December 26, 2007).

Authority, power, and responsibility always go hand-in-hand with each other when they are from God. Legitimate authority is always granted by someone with that authority. It is always accompanied by rules for exercising it and a domain where it can be used. When a person attempts to act on appropriate authority, but has insufficient power, his efforts are futile, and are most likely premature. When a person has the power to do something, but not the authority, then his actions are improper and perhaps illegal or sinful. Even someone with proper authority and power is not free to accomplish the goals any way he pleases. He must work toward his goals responsibly and within the boundaries of what is proper.

These basic ideas are helpful when trying to apply Scripture, because God oftentimes does not explain in detail what is expected of us or how to go about what he desires.

When God tells us that we have certain responsibilities, he is simultaneously saying that he has given us the authority to accomplish them and will supply the power for them. If we do not think we can do it, either we are mistaken or God has yet to impart the power needed and we should seek for it.

If God speaks of our power (or his), it is implicit that it is accompanied by proper authority and its application must be done responsibly. We may need to ask God for guidance on how he wants us to accomplish his goals.

If God refers to authority he has granted us, we still may need to seek God for the power to carry out our responsibility. He will answer these requests at the proper time.

Be careful not to attempt to accomplish something that you do not have the authority to do. Satan may end up being the one that provides the power for its successful completion through which he can exert a measure of control.

39 Homosexuals

Jesus overturned the tables of the moneychangers in the temple area at the beginning[118] and end of his ministry.[119] He was full of righteous anger. Do you have righteous anger about anything?

Sinners enjoyed Jesus' company so much that they invited him into their homes for meals—a very intimate setting in those times.[120]

Jesus was very angry about only one other thing in the gospels: the behavior of some of the religious leaders. One of the worst things the Pharisees were doing was claiming to know God's truth, but then preventing people who did not know the truth from entering the kingdom of God.[121] The attitude of many Christians today is unfortunately accomplishing the same thing.

Some of us have forgotten what we were: *Neither the sexually immoral nor idolaters nor adulterers nor male prostitutes....nor thieves nor the greedy nor drunkards nor slanderers nor swin-*

---
118 John 2:13-17
119 Matthew 21:12-13, Mark 11:15-17, Luke 19:45-46
120 Matthew 9:11
121 Matthew 23:13

*dlers will inherit the kingdom of God. **And that is what some of you were.*** (1 Corinthians 6:9-11, NIV, bold added) Christians are forgiven sinners (and still have a sin nature at that[122]).

Regarding our treatment of non-Christian sinners, Paul wrote: *I have written you in my letter not to associate with sexually immoral people—**not at all meaning the people of this world*** [Ed: i.e., non-Christians] *who are immoral, or the greedy and swindlers, or idolaters. In that case you would have to leave this world....**What business is it of mine to judge those outside the church?*** *Are you not to judge those inside? God will judge those outside...* (1 Corinthians 5:9-13, NIV, bold added) Do you expect non-Christians to behave like Christians? God doesn't.[123]

However, what if a homosexual is, or wants to become, a follower of Jesus Christ? Is it possible to be a follower of Jesus Christ and a homosexual at the same time? If you believe being a homosexual is sinful, is not an equivalent question, *Is it possible to be a follower of Jesus Christ and a sinner at the same time*? Much Scripture is devoted to this question, but one might summarize it exactly as John did in 1 John 1:9 (NIV): *If we confess our sins, he is faithful and just and will forgive us our sins and purify us from all unrighteousness.* The only part of that verse that assigns a responsibility to us is *confess our sins*. God does the rest.

The Biblical definition of *confess* is slightly different than its modern, common usage. In the New Testament, it refers to agreeing in a meaningful way with God about how he views a matter. If agreeing with God that something is a sin throws you into a wrestling match with yourself and Scripture, then you are probably on the right track. All devoted followers of Jesus Christ have

---
122 Romans 13:14, 1 John 1:8,10
123 Romans 2:12-15

experienced that.

If a person believes he is a homosexual by nature, then that person has the opportunity to confess it to God as a sinful condition, but leave it to God to do what he wants to about it. It is at that point that God's forgiveness is complete. God may show the person something he should do, but it is not so that forgiveness may be attained.

Believing one is homosexual by nature is different than homosexual sexual activity, which are actions, and hence, can be *repented* of—that is confessed and turned away from.

Although homosexual sexual acts are sinful[124], take careful note that whether an action is an intentional sin or not really depends on the person's heart condition, which only God knows (and sometimes reveals to the person). *Dwelling upon and nurturing* lustful thoughts, instead of ejecting them from our minds, is unwise, and possibly sinful, regardless of sexual orientation.[125]

Many people fear having to interact with a homosexual—probably stemming from the fear of having to deal with a homosexual displaying more than a friendly interest in them. Much of the fear we have in our lives is simply from feeling unable to handle a hypothetical situation—a situation that may or may not ever occur. It is natural for us to project our feelings onto the people who might trigger those feelings, even though our feelings are a result of what is in us, not what is in them.

Deciding in advance how to handle various interactions with homosexuals in a Christlike way can be very helpful. People that reduce their fear and aversion of homosexuals or anything else may be blessed to discover God's love through more *human be-*

---
124 Leviticus 18:22, Leviticus 20:13, Romans 1:26-27
125 Matthew 5:28, Matthew 15:19 regarding *thoughts*, Philippians 4:8

ings regardless of which sins they commit.

God does not have *revulsion* for homosexuals, he has incredibly awesome *LOVE* greater than we can imagine. If someone has revulsion for homosexuals, it is undoubtedly a result of social and cultural upbringing—or even spiritual blindness or religious training—but it is not from God.

Christians need to be careful of their attitudes and behavior. *...do you dishonor God by breaking the law? As it is written: "God's name is blasphemed among the Gentiles because of you."* (Romans 2:23-24, NIV)

Lastly, it is necessary to recognize that God has set a higher standard for living for *Christian leaders.*[126] (See *Leadership Responsibility.*) Sexually active homosexuals should not be in Christian leadership positions, just as those in uncommitted heterosexual sexual relationships should not be in such positions. They are endangering their spiritual health, and should not be in a role where they can endanger others' as well, but that doesn't mean God rejects them. *Many* Christians are not prepared by God for leadership roles.

*... Jesus stood and said in a loud voice, "If **anyone** is thirsty, let him come to me and drink. **Whoever** believes in me, as the Scripture has said, streams of living water will flow from within him."* (John 7:37-38, NIV, bold added)

---

[126] Acts 6:3, 1 Timothy 3:1-13

40 Leadership Responsibility

Scripture has a lot to say about leadership, and has many examples of both good and bad leaders. A leader is someone in a position of greater authority with responsibilities that extend beyond himself. The Holy Spirit, through the apostle Paul, teaches us that all authority is derived from God and God expects us to submit to leaders that have legitimate authority.[127] With Godly authority, leaders also have greater responsibility and greater power. (See also *Authority, Power, and Responsibility*.) It is appropriate to view this greater responsibility as a call by God to more significant stewardship. A leader's greater power enables him to do more good—or more evil, and hence his potential reward—or punishment—is greater.[128]

Moses led the Israelites for 40 years in the desert with the goal of entering the Promised Land. Instead of reaching his goal, God

---
127 Romans 13:1-7, 1 Peter 5:5
128 Matthew 25:14-30

Leadership Responsibility

told him that he was instead going to die, because he sinned in front of all Israel.[129] God's punishment could not have been much more severe, but it was in line with Moses' sin. Moses, who was the voice of God, and through whom God did miracles, demonstrated such rebelliousness and rejection of God that God would have killed him on the spot had he been anyone else.[130]

The ability to lead is a *gift* from God.[131] Some people seem to be born to be leaders, others benefit from training to an unusually great degree. Sometimes the gift of leadership is imparted overtly by God.[132]

A prudent person will not want to be a leader unless God has granted him the abilities needed to do a good job. Allowing oneself to come into a position of power without the wisdom needed (or discipline to use it) can have devastating effects on himself and others.[133] (In some cases, the responsibility for a leader's failures is shared with, or can be entirely assigned to, the person that put him in his position of leadership.)

In 1 Peter 5:3 we see that church elders are to be examples to the rest of the church. This is one of the greatest responsibilities of a person in a leadership position. Whether a leader is viewed as an example for character and behavior depends on the person doing the viewing. The leader may not have much choice about it.

A role in which we all have an aspect of leadership is in our behavior as Christians. As people claiming to be followers of Christ, we are watched to see what it means to us to be a follower

---

129 Deuteronomy 32:48-52
130 Leviticus 10:1-2, Numbers 16:28-35
131 Romans 12:8
132 2 Timothy 1:6: Paul does not explicitly name the gift that Timothy received, but we see it included leadership qualities in 2 Timothy 1:7.
133 2 Samual 24

of Jesus. We must be careful to not exalt ourselves.[134] God will do that at the proper time.

The more people that see you and know you are a Christian, the greater your accountability to live a life pleasing to the Lord—a holy and pure life.[135] It is appropriate and necessary for church elders that fall into habitual sin to excuse themselves from their role until they once again have a solid foundation of a pure walk with Christ (usually measured in years). The discipline God has commanded for elders caught sinning can destroy a church, and yet, it is the least worst response to it.[136] It is not true that what is done in the privacy of one's own home does not affect others. Everything that a person experiences affects him in some way, and therefore indirectly affects others. However, spiritually, the sins of those in authority *directly* causes harm to those under their care.[137] (See also *The Community Connection*.)

This significant level of Godliness is not a requirement for non-elders. The church is supposed to be a place where people can grow in Christ. God expects elders to have experienced the victory over destructive patterns of behavior. One of their tasks is to help others achieve victory over habitual sin. God has these higher standards for people that are examples to his flock, who also are the people that represent the church (and hence, God) to the community.[138] They must carry a greater weight, and will be rewarded accordingly.[139]

---

134 Matthew 23:12, Luke 14:11, 18:14
135 Romans 2:24
136 1 Timothy 5:19-20
137 2 Samual 24, et al.
138 1 Timothy 3:1-13
139 1 Timothy 5:17-18

41 The Good News

Evangelism is extremely difficult for many Christians. They see how easy it is for some people in their church to share their salvation story or explain the Good News, and it becomes a performance standard they think are supposed to meet—but that is not the case.

God prepares you for whatever he calls you to do. There is no reason to be afraid of poor performance for God. You are his child, and he will help you along with baby steps if that is what you need. We see in Ephesians 4:11-13 that part of being helped along is to come from the more spiritually mature people in God's church. You are to be trained according to the gifts and abilities that God has given you.

Evangelism needs to be conducted thoughtfully. An explanation of God's requirements for Christian living is not evangelism. It is sad to see so many non-Christians viewing Christianity as a religion for self-righteous, condemning people—and, unfortunately, they have cause to think this.

While the Bible refers to the *Good News* and talks at length about it, there is not any particular passage that identifies exactly what it is—or rather, there are many passages that imply different things about what it is.

A basic statement of the Good News is simply: **God has forgiven everyone their offenses against him through the sacrifice of his son, Jesus Christ!**

Some Scripture passages are tied more to the coming of God's righteous kingdom. The Good News might be understood among oppressed people as: **God has come to earth to rescue you!**

The people in Biblical cultures did not need to be told that *God really exists* or that *God has the right to judge you*, and mostly did not need to be told God *is going to judge you for your life*. While these may not technically be part of the Good News, people in our culture may require an explanation of them so they can understand the Good News.

If one strives for a concise, yet complete, statement of the Good News, it should include God's rescue of us from death, which is, not surprisingly, explained along with Jesus Christ's resurrection: **God, who will judge the living and the dead, sent his son, Jesus Christ, to die for us to pay for every wrong thing we have done, and we are now forgiven. God raised Jesus Christ to life to demonstrate his promise to raise us all from the dead and to live with him in joy and peace forever and ever.**

Remember, the Good News is *good* news!

See also *Salvation*.

42 Two Kinds of Faith

It requires wisdom from God to be able to evaluate one's own faith. We tend to think too little or too much of our faith in God. In part this is because we do not know ourselves. As we accumulate decades of life, and as God reveals, we come to understand ourselves better. We may also evaluate our faith poorly because of a lack of understanding of what faith is. (See also *What Is Faith, Really?*)

There are many kinds of faith. Faith is not a black and white matter; it is a grand kaleidoscope of colors, always shifting and changing. Each of us has a certain amount of faith that the sun will rise tomorrow. (The sun rises even if it is cloudy.) Even if you cannot perceive your faith for that, it is likely that it is very great, since faith is based on the experience of evidence. We all have a vast array of experience that has shown us that the sun rises very reliably. We plan for tomorrow as if the sun will rise as it usually does. Would you place a flashlight in the bag you take to school or work *in case the sun does not rise?*

We have a certain amount of faith for every different future event. The faith for each varies. We do not just have one kind of faith for everything. We also have differing amounts of faith in God's various promises. We do not just have a single faith for anything God might do.

However, when it comes to faith for salvation, the landscape of faith can be classified into two kinds: *partial faith* and *saving faith*. We learn about these two kinds of faith in a tour de force exposition in James 2:14-26.

If you were visiting my house and I told you that a meteorite might crash through the roof and smash into you, you might believe, yes, it is possible. But you would not really believe it is going to happen while you are visiting—the chances are just too small.

However, if I said that I just got a phone call from my sky-watching, astronomy professor neighbor and he said that a shower of large meteorites was going to crash onto our property within a few minutes, how would you respond?

If you did not believe me, you might chuckle and sit down and ask for a soda. If you realized you had no reason to disbelieve any of what I said, and felt that it very well may happen, and so looked out the window with some anxiety, you would be expressing a limited kind of faith—possibly *intellectual assent* if you agreed that the evidence was good. **By every measure you give yourself, you might say that you believe what I told you.** You might even explain that you would not be looking out the window if you did not believe me. If I waited to see if you could drum up more faith, nothing related to your faith would change. Your faith would only change if the evidence you had changed.

On the other hand, if you dropped what you were holding and went screaming out the front door, then you would be exhibiting

Two Kinds of Faith

saving faith. You *really* did believe in your heart what I told you. You and I would know it because of how you responded. But it was not your action that created the *saving faith*, it was simply the evidence that you believed me from your heart, not just your mind.

If a third person were present and heard everything I had said, and as a result of seeing you run out the front door, decided to play it safe and run out the front door, too, he would be exhibiting faith *in your action*. He would not have *saving faith* in my words. The action does not bring the faith—only God, and possibly that third person, would know if his faith was a result of trying to play it safe, or actually in my warning.

It is the same for receiving your salvation through Jesus Christ. If you really believe that the Bible is correct when it says Jesus is the son of God, died for your sins, rose from the dead, and is seated at the right hand of the Father in heaven, then you will respond with actions that comes from your heart[140], perhaps running around and screaming, *Hallelujah! Thank you, Lord!*[141]

If you receive this good news and so believe you are saved, but do not respond from your heart, then you are exhibiting limited faith. You may have intellectual assent—openness to what the good news says with no logical reason to disbelieve it—but you are not saved; you are deluded if you think you are saved.

The apostle John wrote in 1 John 5:13 (NIV), *I write these things to you who believe in the name of the Son of God so that you may know that you have eternal life.* We can *know* that we are saved. It is the privilege of all of those who yield control of their life to Jesus. It is part of what brings us peace in this life. It is es-

---
140   Romans 10:9-10
141   The thief demonstrated his saving faith by his words in Luke 23:39-43.

sential for a growing faith in God.

Realize that while it is our responsibility to respond to God's good news of salvation with belief (like an innocent child would upon hearing it), we need his help to do even that.[142] If you desire God's salvation and are willing to yield your life to him, but remain uncertain if you are really saved, it is totally appropriate to ask God to grant you to know that you are saved like the apostle John said. God may need to sort out some matters in your heart and mind before you can *know* you are saved, but ask and keep asking.[143] God will answer that prayer.

You may need to rearrange priorities in your life so you are being obedient to God, because if God is not your Lord[144], he is not your savior. God may use your actions or inactions to show you what is really in your heart. (But it will not be your actions that save you, as explained above.)

Note that *knowing* you are saved is simply a deeper form of *saving faith*. It took the author a year of reading the Bible an hour a day to receive *saving faith*, and then more than another year of devotion to Christ to *know* he was saved. What it will take is unique to each person.

---

142   John 6:44, Ephesians 2:8
143   Luke 11:5-13
144   God is your *lord* when you have yielded control of your life to him and really mean it.

43 The Cross

It is suprising, if not shocking, to discover that some people believe the Bible condones slavery. God did not detail a plan that humans should follow to end all wars, but does anyone believe that God thinks war is a good idea? In fact, there is no plan that humans can successfully follow to end *all* slavery and war. God himself is needed to accomplish those—and he will accomplish them at the proper time.[145]

In the same way, God himself was and is needed to deliver people from slavery to sin. It is not something we can do on our own. Whole books can be written to explain what Jesus did for us on the cross and by his resurrection. One of the things Jesus did is overcome death and retake the authority humans, through sinning, gave Satan and by which he used to be able to control us. The work to deliver us from Satan was completed on the cross; nothing more needs to be done.[146]

The spiritual war that remains on earth is not what many

---

145   1 Corinthians 15:24-26, Hebrews 2:8
146   John 12:31, 16:11

Christians think. Our war is against being deceived, and we win battles by learning, knowing, and understanding the truth. We also need God to give us faith in the truth. (See *Two Kinds of Faith*.) Satan no longer has *authority* over us, but he is still present on earth, and one of the activities he is engaged in is to use his power, illegally, to spread and maintain deceptions in Christians. Then when we believe a lie, we are doing what it takes to tap into the power of Satan and he is able to affect us, in spite of him lacking the authority to do so. When we believe the truth, we tap into the power of God, and receive the effect of that truth, which includes, among other things, deliverance from Satan's lies.

Jesus did not just die so that we could be freed from slavery to sin; he died on the cross so we could be freed from slavery to *everything*. That includes addictions, evil thoughts, and even death. It includes human slave owners, our aging bodies, and everything that forces us to do something other than what we choose to do.

If you are not experiencing this enormously broad freedom, it is because you either (a) are trying to accomplish things outside of God's will, (b) are not asking for or accepting God's help for the things that are too big for you to handle by yourself, or (c) are deceived in some manner. (Note that we will all remain partially deceived until we depart this earth.)

It is important to understand that deceptions and lies do not just pertain to knowledge. We often think of lies as *incorrect facts*, but they much more serious than that. A better name for deception and lies is *spiritual blindness*. This blindness effect can affect anything in all creation,[147] not just the things you know. Liberation from spiritual deception is something that we need God's help for. Fortunately, he gives it generously. Not only did we need Jesus to

---

147 Romans 8:20-22, 1 Corinthians 2:14

die for us, but we need God to enable us to believe that Jesus died for us.[148] A perfectly good prayer for an Atheist or someone who still wonders if they are saved is: *God, if you are real, please enable me to fully believe in Jesus Christ to receive your salvation.*

Paul uses the word *veil* for a kind of spiritual blindness in 2 Corinthians 3:14-17 (NIV): *But their minds were made dull, for to this day the same veil remains when the old covenant is read. It has not been removed, because only in Christ is it taken away. Even to this day when Moses is read, a veil covers their hearts. But whenever anyone turns to the Lord, the veil is taken away. Now the Lord is the Spirit, and where the Spirit of the Lord is, there is freedom.*

Spiritual blindness in our fallen world could cause scientists (and non-scientists) to look at layers of canyon sediment and draw incorrect conclusions about the eras those layers represented. The concrete results of careful scientific inestigation and what we see with our eyes are not immune to the powerful effects of spiritual blindness.[149] A corrupt chain of logic can seem like a trustworthy chain of logic. An incorrect line of human reasoning and deduction can seem like a correct one. It can cause people to see light, goodness, and truth, when in fact they are staring Satan in the face.[150]

---

148 John 6:44, Ephesians 2:8
149 As a result of judgment: John 12:37 in vss. 37-40, Regarding Satan's power: 2 Corinthians 4:4, Regarding the effects of sin: 1 John 2:11
150 2 Corinthians 11:14-15. Also, Satan not quite succeeding in Mark 13:22.

44 Salvation

See also *Need For Forgiveness* and *Two Kinds of Faith*.

Salvation and *being saved* are two of the terms often used to describe being "right" with God. Other phrases that are sometimes used are *received Jesus* or *born again*. Each phrase has its own particular nuance, but the primary meaning of each is the same: *I have no sin in my account with God.*

Every person either has not yet been forgiven by God or is entirely forgiven by God.

Amazingly, the state of being forgiven also affects all sins that will be committed, but have not yet been committed. This is difficult to understand sometimes, but it is easier if one accepts that at the moment of receiving God's forgiveness for all sins, God also transforms the person's nature to no longer be what it once was, but rather to have a new nature that is merged in some mysterious way with God himself. Our thoughts and behavior are not transformed instantly—that is a process, and while we live in our present bodies we will unfortunately retain a (forgiven) sin nature.[151]

Another point that people sometimes have difficulty with is that they simply cannot believe God would just forgive their sins "like that" in a moment of praying to receive God's forgiveness. This kind of thinking should be shut down whenever it comes into your mind for two reasons:

Firstly, forgiveness is something that entirely resides within the forgiver. Certainly, we are used to making our forgiveness dependent upon, say, the attitude of the person who wronged us, but God is not like that. God requires that this old way of forgiving people be given up and his new way be adopted. We are all expected to forgive everyone for everything, because that is exactly what we need from God—all our sins are horrendous to God, but he gives us exactly what we need: complete forgiveness without regard to how awful the sins are. For some offenses, you may need God's help to forgive someone, and he will definitely give this help to you.

The second reason to dismiss the idea that God forgives your sins so easily is that he has not forgiven your sins easily! God's own justice had to be satisfied before he would forgive all your sins. Grievously, we are not able to satisfy the requirements of God's justice to receive his forgiveness. It is not possible. That is precisely why in his awesome love God sent his son, Jesus Christ, to be born on earth without a sin nature, grow up never sinning, have so much suffering in his life that it become familiar[152], and then be crucified (nailed) to a wooden cross to suffer the most humiliating and torturous death available in that culture.

Jesus' death is the price of justice for your forgiveness. It is

---

151 Romans 7, 13:14 (NIV)
152 Isaiah 53:3

also all the price that is needed. There is no more price to be paid for your forgiveness, and God gladly grants the purchased forgiveness to you. He wanted (and wants) to save you! If there had been any other way to meet the requirements of justice besides Jesus dying for you, God would have done it, but there was not.[153] So he did what was necessary out of his great love for us. God's gift of salvation is a completely free gift, for which we do not owe him anything.

Some people do not have trouble understanding why God can forgive sins so "easily," their difficulty is in understanding why they need forgiveness at all! While this is mainly addressed in *Need For Forgiveness*, it is worth mentioning here that while there are greater and lesser sins[154], the smallest sin still completely soils a person.

---

153 Mark 14:35-36
154 The Law given by Moses dictated various degrees of punishment. *See also* Luke 12:47-48

45 The Personal Relationship

There is a difference between knowing about God and knowing God. One can know *about the God of the Bible* by reading the Bible. To those that are not secure in their belief that God is real, the idea of *knowing God* is nonsense. It is a statement of relationship between two living beings. If God were not real, the only "relationship" one could have with God would be an imaginary (or hallucinatory) relationship. But to those that know Jesus Christ is alive and well today in heaven because He has interacted with them, *knowing God* is a exactly like knowing another person.

When we say that we *know someone*, we are implying a number of things about the relationship:

- We have met.
- We remember each other's names.
- We know something about each other.
- We enjoy talking or doing activities together.

- We are involved in each other's lives to some degree.

Our friendships are not solely based on what we know about our friends. Likewise, you cannot *know God* by *knowing about God*. This is why some Christians tout the importance of our *personal relationship with Jesus Christ*. These Christians have (presumably) interacted with God and have a growing relationship with God just like they would have with a human being. To *know God*, one must have continuing interaction with God. We start out not knowing God very well. After some years, we know him a little. After many years, we may know him very well.

A spiritually healthy Christian will always have *growing faith* in God. There is no such thing as a healthy, but unchanging, relationship with God.[155] The only way to have growing faith in God is by having ongoing personal interactions with God.

Our relationship with God may seem to be slow in its development—partially because God is so complex. God cannot be understood completely,[156] but our understanding can grow. He is simultaneously our heavenly father, lord, king, friend, counselor, helper, and brother—to name a few of the roles that God has in our lives. If you feel like your relationship with God has been rather one-sided—you being obedient, but not hearing from God—begin to pray regularly that God will show you how he is speaking to you and is involved in your life. He will answer that prayer, although when he does depends on many issues. Just make sure you are loving God as best you can.

"Whoever has my commands and obeys them, he is the one

---
155 Revelation 3:15-16
156 Isaiah 55:8-9

who loves me. He who loves me will be loved by my Father, and I too will love him and show myself to him." (John 14:21, NIV)

46 What Is Faith, Really?

First read *The Personal Relationship*.

Few things in the Bible are revealed as being more important than faith. Those who have struggled to understand Biblical faith may have found its deeper meaning to be elusive. Frequently the struggle is no small matter at all. What Christian familiar with the gospels has not striven to understand what faith is when she or a loved one has a serious illness?

There are multiple passages in the gospels where someone is miraculously healed and Jesus says, *Your faith has healed you.* Likewise, there are passages where some miracle is not accomplished and Jesus explains that the cause was *because you have so little faith.* As if that were not enough to try to master, there are also passages where Jesus says, *Just believe*, as if it was a simple thing to do.

Hebrews 11:1 (NIV) says: *Now faith is being sure of what we*

What Is Faith, Really?

hope for and certain of what we do not see. The rest of the chapter gives examples of faith. Take a moment to write down a statement of what faith is in your own words.

Elusive, isn't it? Perhaps frustrating—or even maddening! The reason is that the Bible does not explain what faith is directly other than Hebrews 11:1. The passages that talk about faith do so indirectly. Another reason is that faith-related Bible passages do not usually specify whether the faith in that passage is faith in God, some generic form of faith, or faith in something else, such as a promise of God.

Hebrews 11:1 is a generic definition of faith that can be applied to faith in things other than God. Look at Hebrews 11:1 (NIV) again with bold added: *Now faith is being **sure** of what we hope for and **certain** of what we do not see.*

This is a good supplemental definition: Faith as defined in Hebrews 11:1 is *surety* and *certainty.*

Consider a young child with good parents. If anything threatens or frightens the child, she runs to her parents. If the child is wandering around in a store, you may notice that every now and then she looks to see that her parent is in sight. This gives her a feeling of security and boldness, and usually she continues to explore. If she discovers that her parent is not in sight, she gets a worried look and may begin to cry.

If the child is confused about something or has a question, she looks to her parent for the answer. If the child is hungry, she looks to her parent for food. If the child gets hurt, she goes to a parent.

In Matthew 18:3 (NIV), Jesus says, *And he said: "I tell you the truth, unless you change and become like little children, you will never enter the kingdom of heaven."*

Does the analogy between a child/parent and your relationship with God make it easier to picture what faith is? A child has many needs that she cannot provide for herself. She relies on her parents for so many of her needs that it becomes automatic to look to a parent when she cannot do anything for herself. **It is in this picture that we can see the kind of relationship God wants to have with us.**

Faith is the substance of your relationship with God. It defines your relationship with God. The child's faith in her parents is absolute in the picture story above. Whenever she relies on her parents, they come through for her. To her there is no alternative to relying on her parents for everything. There is no Plan B if her parents do not come through for her. She does not know what to do if she cannot find a parent. If a parent tells the child something that is not inconsistent with her experience, the child simply believes the parent. There is no struggle to believe. This is why Jesus sometimes said *Just believe.* He is encouraging the person to have childlike faith.

When you see God come through on enough of his promises, you will start to have general faith in God. Some people believe that knowledge and understanding are contrary to faith, but that is not true. God gave us our minds to be used[157] and understanding is an essential part of faith. You must first understand the promises of God, otherwise you will put your faith in something not of God, and it very well may not come through for you. A characteristic of all healthy relationships with God is that of growing faith. But it only occurs as you trust God in the promises and commands that you already have, otherwise you are not doing your part for a healthy relationship. God is completely trustworthy; there is never a relationship failure on his part.

---

157   1 Corinthians 2:16, 14:15

What Is Faith, Really?

If you are expecting something from God and it does not happen, consider the young child asking her parent for something. There are many reasons the child might not get what she asked for, but the reason is never because the parent does not love the child. Indeed the parent loves the child and does many things for the child's benefit that the child is not aware of (protection from evil, giving the child experiences to prepare her for the future, etc.).

In God's case, he is afire with such powerful love for his children that his attitude is *ask me for anything and I will give it to you*. The real life restriction on this offer is not, *Is God really willing to give me anything?* The restrictions are *Is this good for my child?* and *Will this cause my child to wander off the good path?* A parent does not give candy to a child every time she wants it, but will occasionally give it to her.

Unfortunately, the reality on earth is that Christians are the front lines in a spiritual war. Not only does God decide what to give his children based on their needs and desires, but also based on the needs of battle. Stronger children are important, and unfortunately, surviving a period of suffering with the Holy Spirit's guidance is one of the best ways to gain strength. If that did not complicate matters enough, God is also ensuring that you grow up into the likeness of Jesus Christ, and is also laying a foundation of blessing for you that will last for all eternity.[158]

So while the child/parent analogy to us/God is very good for helping our understanding our relationship with God, it also tells us that we are only going to understand the things that happen to us like a child can. God sometimes answers our failure to under-

---
158   1 Timothy 6:18-19

stand a situation and our troubled heart with just *trust Me*.[159]

The innermost need of a child is to please her parent. The natural, subconscious response of the child is, *how can I please my parent more?* It is not surprising that we learn that faith is needed to please God: *And without faith it is impossible to please God, ...* (Hebrews 11:6, NIV). In the same way, we ask, *how do I get more faith* or *how can I please God more?* To desire more faith is to desire a deeper relationship with God that is like the earlier child/parent illustration. The first step is to get our eyes off *faith*. We are not looking for faith in faith. We want faith in God, and hence, we need to forget about faith and focus on God. In the illustration, the child is not even capable of understanding what *faith* is. All she knows is her parent.

Ephesians 2:8-9 (NIV) says (bold added), *For it is by grace you have been saved, through faith—and this not from yourselves,* **it is the gift of God**—*not by works, so that no one can boast.*

In Luke 17:4-5, the apostles are surprised that Jesus is telling them to forgive a brother every time if he sins against them seven times in a day and comes back repentant each time. They exclaim *Increase our faith!* (NIV)

Jesus' response in Luke 17:6 amounts to: *you do not need much faith.* He continues in Luke 17:7-10 with a story that might be interpreted as *just do what you are supposed to do.*

Consider your relationships with people. What does it take for them to become deeper and more solid? Where does a child's faith in her parents come from?

All of the instances of the words *trust, faith,* and *belief,* and their variants (like *believe*) in the New Testament (NIV) come from Greek words with the same root. As found in the New Testa-

---
159   John 14:1

ment, *trust*, *faith*, and *belief* are very closely related in meaning. Sometimes it helps to consider a confusing passage by substituting one of those words with another. In particular, try substituting *faith* (usually a reference to *faith in God*) with *trust God*. Try this substitution in these two passages:

Matthew 17:20 (NIV): *...I tell you the truth, if you have faith as small as a mustard seed, you can say to this mountain, 'Move from here to there' and it will move. Nothing will be impossible for you.*

Or Mark 10:52 (NIV): *"Go," said Jesus, "your faith has healed you." Immediately he received his sight and followed Jesus along the road.*

Can you see that what you need to do is *trust God* whether he has chosen to heal you or move a mountain *or not*? Trusting God means you acknowledge that he is in control (and he really is) and he is going to do what is best for you, and sometimes that means suffering.

The common stumbling block here is incorporating the fact of spiritual battle into the relationship incorrectly. The battle is not to receive what God wants to give us, it is the battle to trust God regardless of what happens! Total victory in the spiritual battle is achieved when you trust God regardless of what is happening in your life. Then nothing in all creation can prevent God from moving your mountain or healing you.

Lastly, stop evaluating how strong you think your faith is. For most of us it is *MUCH* weaker than we think. An example that might reveal what it is like to think your faith is good—when it is actually poor—is to consider your faith in what Scripture teaches will happen to you when you die. It is one thing to say you believe that when you die you will go to heaven to be with Jesus and will have inexpressible joy and peace. It is another to face death looking forward to it with joyful anticipation! Perhaps you consider your mortality with fear, or at least with anxiety. This is a faith issue. When you have *strong* faith in God about what he says about death, you will look forward to your natural death.[160] Needless to say, not many of us have that kind of faith.

Do not condemn yourself for weak faith! Sometimes it can be difficult to be joyful—even just accepting—about the faith God has giving you. Thinking something terrible is going to happen (or has happened) because you did not have enough faith can be a source of great, but unwarranted, anxiety. Trust that God gives us the faith we need, and he only expects us to exercise the faith that we do have—not the faith we do not have.[161] Remember that faith is a *gift* from God.[162] If you are called to have strong faith, then when your faith grows to the size of a mustard seed, God will be moving mountains for you. Until then, whenever the question of the degree of your faith comes to mind, replace it with the picture story of a child's relationship with her parent, and just do your part. The only thing the child can do is focus on Jesus Christ, be obedient to him, and make requests—then the relationship will flourish and her faith will grow. This is not a new idea. The apostle John said it over and over.[163]

"Why do you call me, 'Lord, Lord,' and do not do what I say? I will show you what he is like who comes to me and hears my words and puts them into practice. He is like a man building a house, who dug down deep and laid the foundation on rock. When a flood came, the torrent struck that house but could not shake

---

160 Philippians 1:23
161 Romans 12:6
162 Ephesians 2:8-9
163 John 14:23, John 15:10, 1 John 2:5, 1 John 5:3, and 2 John 1:6.

it, because it was well built. But the one who hears my words and does not put them into practice is like a man who built a house on the ground without a foundation. The moment the torrent struck that house, it collapsed and its destruction was complete." (Luke 6:46-49, NIV)

47 Little Gods

A trained and experienced art appraiser can identify a Leonardo Da Vinci painting even if she has never seen it before. This is because a part of the character of the master painter is uniquely expressed in his paintings. Likewise, God created our physical universe and a part of his nature is uniquely expressed in his creation.

Our universe is God's painting—but it is not a priceless painting. God did create something priceless inside the universe though, and it was made in a truer image of God: people. People are priceless because they were given something unique to God: free will. Nothing else in all our world has free will. We are made just like God in more ways than we know. We are very much finite versions of our infinite God. We both have thoughts, feelings, and memory. We both have will, understanding, and power. And we both—God and all people—will exist forever.

You may wonder what the big deal about free will is. After all, God also made the angels and gave them free will—and he could raise up new people out of stones if he wanted to.[164]

Free will is the aspect of our being that allows us to make a moral choice or an immoral choice. The big deal is this: it is the capacity to choose to accept God or choose to reject God. We can be like God or unlike God. We can choose to accept or reject that *God is God and we are not.*

To understand why it is such a big deal to choose God or not choose God it is helpful to have some understanding of God's innate value. See *Inherent Value.*

The fact is that to choose God is *everything.* It is the only perfect choice. It encompasses all goodness, rightness, harmony, and fullness of life. On the flipside, *nothing* is not the opposite of choosing God. Failing to choose God is to choose *emptiness, destruction, pain, and death.* The only middle ground is what we experience today on earth, a mix of goodness and evil—but take note: this situation is temporary. When death comes for you, you will be forced out of this "middle ground" to a place where there is no middle ground. It does not exist. It is like being indoors or outdoors. You cannot be in both. You are either *in* or you are *out.* With God or apart from God.

So while all people are little gods in that they were created like God, only those that choose God are also like him *in spirit.* They choose to follow him and all that is in accordance with his nature. They choose to be *children of God*[165]. God glories in that choice and in whatever way we are incapable of being like him because of sin, he will do for us. That is how God raises up children for himself, who are very much appropriately called *Little Gods.*[166] For almost two thousand years, they have been more commonly

---
164 Matthew 3:9, Luke 3:8
165 John 8:38-44
166 John 10:34-35

known as *Christians*[167]—the people who have chosen to accept God's forgiveness of their sins through Jesus Christ, come into right relationship with him, and have chosen to follow him.

---

[167] Acts 11:26

48   Sin

While we are still very young, a time comes when we know right from wrong.[168] There we begin our life's journey of facing moral choices. At each opportunity, we either choose what is right and good, or choose what is wrong. Scripture reminds us that we have all chosen wrong[169], which is not particularly difficult to accept after discovering God's black and white standard.

Either we are perfect, never having done anything wrong—even in ignorance of God's requirements—or we have not. A *sin* is an offense against God. God requires complete sinlessness to be righteous (*right with him*) in his eyes. The idea that our good must outweigh our bad presumably originated with people struggling to find a reason to believe they are good. This concept is not from God.

If this charge wasn't bad enough, we also have something often called *original sin*. Our original sin is inherited from our ancestors, which they inherited from their ancestors, and so on,

---
168   Isaiah 7:15-16
169   Romans 3:23

back to Adam, who was the first intentional sinner. While there is physical manifestation of this *sin nature*, it is incorrect to think of it as genetic or as a result of child rearing. It is a spiritual condition that we have for being members of Adam's race.

There is no easy way to understand why it is fair that we inherit a sin debt that we, as individuals, did not commit. But it is clear that it is a spiritual reality. (See *The Ancestral Connection* and *The Community Connection*.) It is a normal reaction to look at God's perfect standard and feel it is unfair. No one, or at least woefully few, could ever meet such requirements. We are used to standards created by people where the ability to meet the standard is taken into account when setting the standard. But God did not create this requirement for us. Rather, it is a reflection of his nature that has always existed, not a rule he thought up.

Originally, God and man dwelled together in harmony—in the Garden of Eden.[170] When Adam and Eve sinned, this was no longer possible due to God's nature. At that point, God expressed his nature in several ways:

His *justice* required that Adam's and Eve's death.[171] His *love* gave them the hope of victory over evil[172]. Also out of his *love* for Adam and Eve, and all future mankind, God withdrew from their presence on earth, because the nature of God's presence is such that evil is destroyed.[173] Rather than see mankind destroyed, God chose rather to save us, and so began God's preparation for the coming of our Savior, Jesus Christ, to earth.

See also *Need For Forgiveness* and *Salvation*.

---

170   Genesis 3:8
171   Genesis 3:22
172   Genesis 3:15
173   Exodus 33:20, 1 John 1:5

49 The Ancestral Connection

When studying human fallenness and original sin, inevitably the question arises, *why am I sinful because Adam sinned?* After all, *He* ate from the Tree of Good and Evil and sinned, not me! It is a great question to ask, and one that deserves an answer, since it is part of the reason why we need God's salvation.

The answer may be difficult to accept unless we recognize that we are used to thinking of ourselves as independent individuals because that is what we have been taught and seen demonstrated in our culture. Consider other times and cultures where a man's children would have been treated as special just because their father was a noble. The people of those times would have had less trouble than us accepting the idea that a nobleman's children should be treated with special honor just because they were his children. Today we might do it to avoid annoying a powerful person, but would we do it because the children *deserved* it? If you were royalty, you might very well believe your children deserved special treatment, because *you* were important, and they belong to you and were important to you.

The fact that we were made in God's image has profound meaning. Because God is infinite, in some sense we share in God's infiniteness. The best way to understand what it means to be in God's image is to look to Jesus Christ, about whom Paul wrote, *He is the image of the invisible God, the firstborn over all creation.* (Colossians 1:15, NIV) Hebrews 1:3 (NIV) also tells us, *The Son is the radiance of God's glory and the exact representation of his being,* ...

Throughout the New Testament we see that while God is one God, he exists in three Persons: the Father, the Son, and the Holy Spirit. Jesus said much that helps us understand his relationship to God, the Father, particularly in the book of John. It is a mystery how Jesus can be God and be in relationship with the Father, and all the while there still just be one God. A very good way to understand this aspect of God's nature is to recognize that our one God as well as each Person has the substance of *relationship* within himself. Jesus has the substance of relationship in his nature, as does God, the Father, and it is also found in the relationship between Jesus and the Father.

When God created male and female, he was expressing his image. The qualities in both males and females are derived from God. Our Trinitarian God is best revealed and glorified as a married male and female living in perfect harmony with common purpose. (This helps us understand why homosexuality and divorce are contrary to Godliness.)

The point of this chapter is to say this: God's Trinitarian nature was given to us when we were created in his image. This part of his nature embodies what we call *relationship*. Not just any relationship, but a Father-Son-Holy Spirit relationship. Each of us, both males and females, has within us a part of this same nature—a nature that is best visualized in Scripture as a good father-son relationship. It is such a close, intimate connection that it is properly described as *oneness*.[174]

Amazing as it is, our natures are intertwined with our parents' and children's natures. This is a spiritual reality. The fact that we have similar genes to our parents and children is part of the physical form that this spiritual reality takes. (See also *Cycle of the Spirit*.)

Identical twins are blessed with a special kind of relationship that differs from an, also special, marriage relationship. Twins experience a different aspect of Jesus' and the Father's oneness than a married couple, but we all have this ancestral, relational nature in us.

When Adam sinned and fell, his *nature* was altered. He could no more give birth to sinless children than apes. It was (and is) the nature of the universe derived from God that his children shared in his nature. We see that Nehemiah recognized this when he first prayed to God. He confesses not only his sins, but the sins of his forefathers.[175] We also see the connection when God proclaimed his name to Moses in Exodus 34:7. He revealed that he is a God who maintains blessings to a thousand generations of children for the goodness of an ancestor, and a God who punishes to three or four generations of children for the sins of their ancestor. We also see Jesus reframe something the teachers of the law and Pharisees had said to show them their sinful connection to their ancestors in Matthew 23:30-32.

---

174   John 10:30
175   Nehemiah 1:6-7

It is not a question of fairness that we inherited a sin nature from Adam. We inherited that sin nature because we are privileged to have a nature that includes the relational aspect of God's nature. The apostle Paul reminds us that we all sin in Romans 3:23 (NIV): *for all have sinned and fall short of the glory of God,* ... While we are fallen because of Adam's sin, we also testify that we are Adam's children whenever we sin.

Whenever we trust God, we affirm we are the true children of Abraham, the father of *faith*, because we are his children *in spirit*, whether or not we are biologically descended from him or not.[176] All Christians are children of royalty.[177] Paul expounds at length on how we can no longer live as we once did before we were children of God.[178] We need to be affirming our *oneness* with our spiritual Father (and, when possible, our earthly parents).

Lastly, if you still think it unfair that you inherited Adam's sinful nature, note that the same nature that caused us to have original sin is the same nature that gives us the blessings we have as children of God, as well as the blessings from all of our ancestors back to Adam. We all need to be spiritual children of Abraham to have the faith by which we are saved by God.

---

176 Romans 9:6-8, Galatians 3:6-9
177 Galatians 4:6-7
178 Romans 6-8, esp. 6:1-2 & 6:11-13, Ephesians 4:17

50 The Community Connection

Please first read *The Ancestral Connection.*

Just as there is a very real and powerful spiritual connection with God and our ancestors through the relational nature we have received from God, there is also a real spiritual connection with those in our community. The community connection exists at all levels—with your friends, your family, the people in your church, town, county, state, country, and even the worldwide community of mankind.

Both the gospels of Matthew and Mark contain a short account of a visit Jesus made to his home town of Nazareth. Mark 6:3-6 (NIV, text in brackets added) says, ... And they took offense at him [Jesus]. Jesus said to them, "Only in his hometown, among his relatives and in his own house is a prophet without honor." He could not do any miracles there, except lay his hands on a few sick people and heal them. And he was amazed at their lack of faith.

The passage in Matthew makes it clear why Jesus could not do many miracles: And he did not do many miracles there because of their lack of faith. (Matthew 13:58, NIV)

This last verse often amazes, because God has all the power to do anything he chooses to do. Indeed, a lack of power is never the reason God does not do something. Jesus could not do many miracles in Nazareth for a different reason: he was not wanted there! The people did not want Jesus' healing power. It sounds ridiculous—but that is exactly what a significant absence of faith looks like.

These accounts of Jesus in Nazareth in Matthew and Mark show us the power of a community (family and relatives[179], and a town, in this case): **the community had enough power to stop God from being compassionate and kind among them**.

God talks about how powerful the sins of a community are compared to the righteousness of three of the most righteous people ever to have lived (Noah, Daniel, and Job) in Ezekiel 14:12-23. We see that God judges a community according to what they deserve as well as judges individuals according to what they deserve (salvation in the case of Noah, Daniel, and Job).

In an amazing exchange in Genesis 18:20-33, we see Abraham pressing God not to treat righteous individuals as sinners when God passes judgment on the community they live in. Lot is the only righteous individual there, and God saves him. God was willing to save Lot's family, but some did not have faith, and were destroyed with Sodom and Gomorrah.[180]

In Joshua 7:1 (NIV), we see But the Israelites acted unfaithfully in regard to the devoted things; Achan son of Carmi, the son

---

179 Matthew 13:57, Mark 6:4
180 Genesis 19:14, 26

of Zimri, the son of Zerah, of the tribe of Judah, took some of them. So the LORD's anger burned against Israel. Even though Achan was the only individual that sinned[181] God's view was that all Israel had sinned.

God did not create us to be complete by ourselves. We are only fully complete when fully in God's presence and in community with other Christians. In 1 Corinthians 12, especially verses 12-27, we see that Christians are all parts of God's church body, whether we think we are or not, and whether we think we need anything from the rest of the body or not. God helps clarify one of the consequences of this by commanding that we are not to give up the habit of meeting together with other Christians—that we need each other to encourage one another and to spur each other toward love and good deeds.[182]

In this age of individualism in which many have the financial resources to hire people to do whatever they can not do themselves, it can require a conscious effort to set time aside to nurture our community connections. Fortunately, nurturing our relationships is not always a laborious effort. Set aside and enjoy time with your Christian friends. There is nothing wrong with having relatively superficial relationships, but be willing to allow them to deepen when opportunities arise (sometimes years apart). Many friendships tend to stay at the point of adding a more personal aspect to them. When you are comfortable with it, share some of your struggles or talk more about issues that are important to you (without smiling). Don't expect reciprocal behavior. Go ahead and share what is on your mind even if the other person does not do the same. This will bear fruit at the proper time. Trust grows in

---
181 Joshua 7:20
182 Hebrews 10:24-25

different ways and at different speeds for people.

Don't suggest how someone might solve their problems if they reveal their struggles with you. It can be very difficult to resist this urge for many people, but it is part of a maturing friendship. When the time comes that they value your opinion (it can take years), they will ask for it. **Asking for your opinion in an early-stage friendship is usually because the person is looking for encouragement**, and you might respond with just that. It also can happen if they perceive you have experience in the area they are struggling with. Even so what they usually need is just a better feeling of security. To understand when someone actually wants your opinion, ask yourself, has our relationship developed to the point where they might follow my advice even if they disagree with it? This is a sign of trust and will be present when they actually want your advice!

More precious to a friendship than words of encouragement is taking action, no matter how small. Offering to drop a meal off to someone's family (and meaning it) in a time of crisis is worth more than ten offers of "Let me know if I can help in any way."

With your more mature friendships, learn to lean on them. This is really the beginning of a mature friendship—when you love and trust someone enough to put some of your well being at risk with them.

It is always valuable to keep your friends before God in prayer. Also keep the heads of families and communities before God just as Paul writes to Timothy (and us) in 1 Timothy 2:1-2 (NIV, bold added): *I urge, then, first of all, that requests, prayers, intercession and thanksgiving be made for **everyone**—for **kings** and **all***

those in authority, *that we may live peaceful and quiet lives in all godliness and holiness.*

51 Conception

The word *conception* is a form of the word *concept*. It is no coincidence that God tells Jeremiah something amazing in Jeremiah 1:4-5 (NIV): *Now the word of the LORD came to me saying, "Before I formed you in the womb I knew you, ..."*

Before we were conceived in our mother's womb, we were conceived in the mind of God. Possibly the most important word in this passage is the word that is absent: *about*. God did not say *I knew about you*, or *I decided about you*, he said, *I knew you*. To say *I knew you* is a statement about a relationship between two living beings. (See also *The Personal Relationship*.) Recall that Jesus declared that the resurrection of the dead was real because of a verb tense in the Old Testament.[183]

Isaiah 55:8-9 tells us that God's thoughts are not like our thoughts, but rather his thoughts are higher than our thoughts. Could he mean that we existed in some fashion before we were conceived in our mothers' wombs? Yes, he could. God tells us something about us after we have become Christians in Colos-

---
[183] Mark 12:26-27

sians 3:3-4 (NIV): *For you died, and your life is now hidden with Christ in God. When Christ, who is your life, appears, then you also will appear with him in glory.* The reference to our death is a reference to our *old man*[184] being gone since we are born again as a new creation in Christ—an eternal Christ that existed before we were conceived..

What does it mean that Christians were somehow alive before our parents were born? I have no idea. But the passages above do point out that our lives are something greater than our biology. One cannot examine a fetus to determine when our lives began, because our lives transcend the physical realm.

Trying to define when a sperm and embryo become a human, and hence worthy of having their lives protected by our laws, is an effort to pin down the arbitrary. Science understands the process of sperm and embryo being transformed into a fetus, then a child, then an adult, and then a dying adult. It is not a scientific endeavor to label some of these *human* and some not. If we wanted to we could say that children are not human until they turn 18 years old. Science can not argue for or against it. It is a philosophical and religious debate as to when a sperm and embryo becomes human.

Since the basis of our belief that abortion kills a human being is Biblical and not scientific, can we expect non-religious people to ever accept God's viewpoint? (Note that an abortion is not *murder* if the father, mother, and doctor believe the fetus is not *human*, but it is still a sin, since it destroys God's work and God's plans.[185])

The only avenue open to Christians is legally influencing laws to be according to our faith. This will only happen when

---

184 2 Corinthians 5:17
185 Job 31:15, Psalm 139:13, Isaiah 44:2, 24, 49:5, Jeremiah 1:5

sufficient numbers of people agree with God's view. This may not ever happen, but we are not without hope. God himself provides the answer to our predicament in 2 Chronicles 7:14 (NIV): *if my people, who are called by my name, will humble themselves and pray and seek my face and turn from their wicked ways, then will I hear from heaven and will forgive their sin and will heal their land.*

Is it a surprise to see the responsibility for abortion in our country squarely on Christian shoulders? It shouldn't be. God is always more powerfully present wherever he finds faith in him. (See also *The Community Connection*.) There is no other way to bring the power of God to bear on our problems than through our faith. Praise God that he is willing to do this for our land. Imagine how little hope we would have if we had to rely on non-Christians to stop abortions.

52 Atheism, The New Religion

re·li·gion [ri-**lij**-*uh* n] –*noun* 1. a set of beliefs concerning the cause, nature, and purpose of the universe[186]

a·the·ism [**ey**-thee-iz-*uh* m] –*noun* 1. the doctrine or belief that there is no God.[187]

When it was unpopular to be an Atheist, you did not hear much about them. Now that science has expanded into every area of our lives, Atheistic beliefs are easier to defend and are in the news more. There was a recent article in *Time* magazine about

---

186 religion. Dictionary.com. *Dictionary.com Unabridged (v 1.1)*. Random House, Inc. http://dictionary.reference.com/browse/religion (accessed November 19, 2007)
187 atheism. Dictionary.com. *Dictionary.com Unabridged (v 1.1)*. Random House, Inc. http://dictionary.reference.com/browse/atheism (accessed: November 19, 2007).

Atheists sending their kids to Atheist "Sunday School"[188] to learn values.

We are a politically Atheistic society; just look at how many political candidates win elections who explain their political beliefs as being rooted in Jesus Christ. Being so overtly religious is usually a political death knell in American (and other industrialized countries') politics.

But do not blame the Atheists. God himself is *very* attractive. The more you know God, the more you love him. It is Christians that have made Christianity unattractive. To make matters worse many Christians have embraced parts of science as the source of ultimate truth.

> sci·ence [**sahy**-*uh* ns] –*noun* 2. systematic knowledge of the physical or material world gained through observation and experimentation[189]

Science is not *evil*. What is wrong is replacing trust in God with trust in science. Every scientific measurement indicates that after death, a person's consciousness is gone. However, God has much to say about life after death, including that a person's consciousness continues (as well as memory, thoughts, and feelings).[190] To what degree do you trust each?

Science is glorious! It is the study of God's divine creation, just as the medical arts are the study of God's greatest creation—

---

188   *Sunday School for Atheists.* Time Magazine, page 99, December 3, 2007.
189   science. Dictionary.com. *Dictionary.com Unabridged (v 1.1).* Random House, Inc. http://dictionary.reference.com/browse/science (accessed: November 19, 2007).
190   Luke 16:19-31

people.[191] But, by definition, science can not see into the spiritual world. If we could detect the objects of our faith scientifically, then we would no longer need to have *faith*. And God will not allow that to happen, because it would undermine the way people are saved—that is, through faith.[192] See also *Salvation* and *What is Faith, Really?*

---

191 1 Timothy 4:4, 6:17
192 See *Is God Real?*

53 Such Pain and Suffering

Please first read *Little Gods*.

In an effort to try to understand God better, sometimes the author thinks of God using his right hand to carry out his conscious decisions. Examples of this would be when he speaks to people, passes judgment on some matter, and when he gives you the best parking space at a crowded football game.

His left hand, then, is what he uses to run the day-to-day operations of the universe. When you have a ball in your palm-down hand and open your fingers, do you think God decides at that moment that it would be a good idea to use gravity to pull the ball out of your hand and send it toward the ground? I do not know, but completely reliable results of actions (e.g., laws of physics) the author attributes to God's left hand—the nature of the universe that is upheld by God.[193]

---

193   Colossians 1:17, Hebrews 1:3

Romans 5:13-14 (NIV): ... *before the law was given, sin was in the world. But sin is not taken into account when there is no law. Nevertheless, death reigned from the time of Adam to the time of Moses, even over those who did not sin by breaking a command ...*

This can be a confusing passage because it speaks about two separate things: the relationship of a person with God (a right-hand interaction) and the natural effects of sin (a left-hand interaction). It says that people who did something that was a sin—before the command was given that let the person know it was a sin—have not harmed their relationship with God (*But sin is not taken into account when there is no law.*) Then it says that because of the nature of the universe, the results of that sin were still death.[194]

Sometimes it is difficult, if not impossible, to understand why God allows such pain, suffering, and evil that we have on earth. The author believes it is accurate to think of this as God's left hand at work. They are the *natural* consequence of sin on earth. God is grieving with his right hand, but he does not usually stop the natural order of things even though there is such pain. Remember this: God made the universe work the way it works and he made no mistakes. All the problems, sin, and pain on earth are a result of the actions of people.

His promise is to be with us at such times, and whether we perceive it or not, he helps us through those times.[195] The best time to learn of God's love is not when we are in anguish. We need to build and keep building our relationship with God whenever we can. We need to be *followers* of Jesus Christ who are in motion, not just static *Christians*.[196]

---

194 *See also* Romans 6:23
195 Hebrews 13:5-6
196 Matthew 7:24-27, Luke 6:46-49

When in the depths of pain, give grace to yourself to let God minister to you. Remember he came to serve as well as teach us how to serve. Let him serve you when you have done what you can for yourself and with the help you can get from other people.[197]

While God is the number one upholder of the consequences of actions (which is what makes our free will meaningful), remember he is also the number one upholder of salvation from the natural, but painful, consequences of our actions. He is our eternal Savior and will deliver us from every evil and all pain.

---

197   Matthew 20:28, Mark 10:45, John 14:15-18, 26, 16:13-14

54 God: Person or Machine?

Is it always wrong to resist God? There are many passages in the Bible where people—often Godly leaders—plead to the Lord for him to do something other than what he has said he will do. Should we not instead be swift to submit to the Lord all of the time?[198]

Sometimes without realizing it, we think of God as a machine instead of a person. This can very easily lead us to respond to God as if he were a machine. For example, God reliably causes his sun to rise each day.[199] We count on the sun rising each day as if a machine were controlling it, since our experience with people, who are ever growing and changing, may not have given us too many examples of such complete reliability. We may never think to thank God for making his sun rise, because we do not perceive the sun as a daily, intentional blessing from God to us.

198 Matthew 21:28-32, James 4:7
199 Matthew 5:45

Sometimes it is helpful to think of God's machine-like behavior as his *left hand* at work, and his more person-like qualities as his *right hand* at work. (See also *Such Pain and Suffering*.) But it is more accurate to separate God's creation from God himself. *Pantheistic* beliefs are those that identify God with the universe and nature. In fact the universe and nature *are* made in God's image, so we can see him in nature in some ways, but the key difference is: God is separate from his creation. (See also *Little Gods*.) The work of God's left hand can more accurately be described as God's creation operating as he designed it to. While God's presence is required so his creation continues to function,[200] he is not a part of it. While mankind can manipulate God's creation, we can not manipulate God.

God almost always describes himself as a person with great power and authority and not as a machine. Jesus Christ, after all, is the exact representation of God,[201] and he was always person-like in his behavior in the Bible. Our susceptibility to attribute machine-like qualities to God comes from the limitations inherent a relationship which begins with us hearing and reading *about* God. To find our true God—a God without rules or regulations, except the "law" to love one another,[202] we must look to him as a person—a kind and generous person with whom we can ask for blessings even if such requests are not specifically modeled in the Bible. He is a great and mighty person whom we can know—like a person. (See also *The Personal Relationship*.)

Regarding whether it is always wrong to resist God's will, the answer can only be found in considering God as he is—a Per-

---
200 Colossians 1:17
201 Hebrews 1:3
202 John 1:17, 13:34, Romans 8:2, 10:4, 13:8-10, Galatians 2:16, 3:24, 5:14, 6:1-2, Philippians 3:9, 2 John 1:5

son—not a machine. A machine-like response is that it is always wrong to resist God's will, and the issue really is, do we know his will well enough to just obey without arguing with him or seeking him further? The better approach is to consider God as our heavenly Father, just as Jesus taught.[203]

As a Person, God is very *un*machine-like. He is unpredictable and his ways and thoughts are inscrutable.[204] He sometimes hides matters from us[205] and sometimes tests us so we may learn about ourselves. We often spend a huge amount of energy trying to find peace by trying to understand what God is or is not doing or what he will or will not do—but we should not and cannot find a sense of security in God's predictability.

We need to find our sense of security from God in knowing what kind of person he is and what it means that he loves us, not in understanding what he will or won't do in every situation. Since God is a Person, we *can* argue with him and ask him questions, without fearing that such behavior is sinful. God wants us to interact with him. He wants to be involved in every part of your life. He loves you and wants to help and bless you!

---

203 Mathew 6:9
204 Isaiah 55:8-9
205 Proverbs 25:2

55 Outthinking the Bible

Hebrews 7:15-16 (NIV, bold added): *And what we have said is even more clear if another priest like Melchizedek appears, one who **has become a priest** not on the basis of a regulation as to his ancestry but **on the basis of the power of an indestructible life**.*

Hebrews 7:17 (NIV) follows: *For it is declared: "You are a priest forever, in the order of Melchizedek."*

Verse 17 contains the reason (***For*** *it is declared...*) that the writer of Hebrews believes the bolded phrases in verses 15-16. However, to my mind, being immortal is not a requirement to become a priest (e.g., Old Testament Levitical priests). It simply explains the possible duration of the priesthood.

This kind of reasoning is an effort to "outthink the Bible." It happens when a new piece of information is inconsistent with what we already know. Sometimes it happens when we don't understand the new piece of information properly, but a more difficult situation occurs when our understanding of it is incomplete.

In the example above, the new piece of information is: immortality is the basis for priesthood under the New Covenant. The incorrect understanding is: the kinds of things that might qualify someone for a priesthood do not include immortality, which is just an indicator of how long someone could remain a priest.

Trying to reconcile a new piece of information into our understanding can feel like trying to pound a square peg into a round hole. We try and try, but it just won't go! But we can't outthink the Bible. Rather, the Bible is our source of understanding. The right path to understanding this passage comes from taking a step back and accepting that our current understanding of it may be incorrect or incomplete.

This makes it much easier to examine the new piece of information, and tell ourselves that what the Bible is teaching us is that the new piece of information *is true*. So we ask ourselves, *what do I believe that conflicts with this?* When we can identify what the conflict is, the hard part is over. We need only ask God or a person who understands the topic to help us understand the passage better.

Another example:

The idea that we share in the sins (and blessings) of our ancestors can be quite a foreign idea to some, especially where the rights of individuals are held in high esteem. (See also *The Ancestral Connection*.) The author was once in a group of people that was asking each other, is there really such a thing as spiritual inheritance from our human parents? Or is what the Bible implies about that inheritance just genetics and environment?

The group could very well have been trying to understand

what God meant when he said in Exodus 20:5-6 (NIV, text in brackets added): *... for I, the LORD your God, am a jealous God, punishing the children for the sin of the fathers to the third and fourth generation of those who hate me, but showing love to a thousand* [generations] *of those who love me and keep my commandments.*

The group was essentially trying to understand what the mechanism was by which God punished and blessed children. While that is a noble goal, the thinking the group started with could have been better. The group should have first accepted that Exodus 20:5-6 is telling us that spiritual inheritance is real. The fact that God is punishing and blessing children because of their ancestors defines the existence of spiritual inheritance. Then a more appropriate question would have followed such as: Are there examples in the Bible where we can see a spiritual inheritance at work that is not the result of genetics or the environment?

In the first example (the text before *Another example*), there is a questionable leap of logic from what Hebrews 7:15-16 says and the assertion that immortality doesn't seem to be a requirement for becoming a priest.

When we are studying the Bible, it sometimes helps to remember some of our high school grammar. When trying to understand a long sentence, it can help to first identify the main actors in it. To do this, one thing we can do is eliminate prepositional phrases. In the passage, *one who has become a priest ... on the basis of the power of an indestructible life,* we can eliminate *of an indestructible life* to see that the qualification for being a priest is not *an indestructible life*, but rather a *power*. A less detailed version of the passage that would still be correct is, *one who has become a priest ... on the basis of the power.*

The qualification for priesthood that the writer of Hebrews is talking about is not immortality, it is a power which is the source of an indestructible life. But this power may do other things as well. What the power is exactly is not given by the writer of Hebrews, but we can ask ourselves, what power is it that could grant an indestructible life? Whatever it is, having that power is what the writer of Hebrews is telling us is what qualifies one to be a priest. (It's a good bet that it is a power that is from God.)

When your understanding of a passage depends on a single word—in this case we eliminated a phrase because it started with the word *of* to try to understand it better—a quick word study may be called for. In this case, we would like to see if *indestructible life* also modifies the word *power* in the original language. If it didn't, then our original understanding that the requirement for being a priest was an indestructible life might have been better.

We must learn how to study the Bible, because then we will not try to outthink its truths, but rather will enjoy learning from God through it.

Part III

56 Cycle of the Spirit

What do the bolded portions of these three passages have in common?

> *They serve at a **sanctuary that is a copy and shadow of what is in heaven**. This is why Moses was warned when he was about to build the tabernacle: "See to it that you make everything according to the pattern shown you on the mountain."* (Hebrews 8:5, NIV, bold added)

> *For all the Prophets and the Law prophesied until John. And if you are willing to accept it, **he is the Elijah who was to come**.* (Matthew 11:13-14, NIV, bold added)

> *For **my flesh is real food and my blood is real drink**. Whoever eats my flesh and drinks my blood remains in me, and I in him.* (John 6:55-56, NIV, bold added)

Have you ever wondered about the meaning of any of these

passages? **They all speak about things that are real in the spiritual realm by referring to things in the physical realm.**[206] In the first case, we find out there is a temple in heaven that looks like the one God described for Moses to build—but the one in heaven is not the copy, the one on earth is. In the second case, Jesus tells his listeners that John the Baptist *is* the Elijah that was prophesied to come.[207] In the third case Jesus doesn't say his flesh and blood *represent* food and drink, he says they *are* real food and drink.

If we had examined the molecules of Jesus body when he was on earth, we would have found them to be that of human flesh. However, the full truth about what they were includes their invisible, spiritual qualities.

Note that this is different than *symbolic representation*. A symbol is something used to represent something else, where there is no actual link between a symbol and its object—the link between a symbol and its object is merely conceptual—a notion in our minds.

When Jesus states that John the Baptist was the prophesied Elijah, he is not saying that John the Baptist is like Elijah, but that he *is* the Elijah in some invisible way—*in spirit*.

There are many things that are true *in spirit* that are revealed in our physical realm—in fact, everything in the physical realm has spiritual connections. (God has certain ownership rights to everything, for example.[208])

Some spiritual realities are eternal, and they may be represented in our physical realm on many occasions in similar or different ways (i.e., a *spiritual cycle*). The spirit of Elijah is something partially derived from God. Whatever that is, it is unchanging and

---

206 John 6:63
207 Malachi 4:5-6
208 1 Corinthians 10:25-26

eternal. It was revealed in Elijah himself as well as in John the Baptist. It may be present today on earth in a person or something else, such as an organization carrying on Elijah-like activities.

Again, this is not a symbolic representation. One can not create an organization carrying on Elijah-like activities and assume it has *the* spirit of Elijah. Spiritual connections are something that exist as a facet of their God-created natures.

There is sometimes disagreement about the purpose of prophetic passages in the Bible—was it just for the hearers at the time the prophecy was given, or is it also true for later readers as well? Determining whether the prophecies are part of an unchanging spirit can help resolve that.

God's nature is that of a savior, so the entirety of his salvation is not found in that Jesus came to earth to save us. Although our relationship with God has him willing to save us through Jesus alone, he is willing to save us from anything in any circumstance all through time. He may use people or things in the physical realm; he may use ideas, emotions, prayer, or worship. Anything in the physical can be connected with God's saving spirit if he chooses. The point is that the saving spirit is a part of God's spirit, which always will exist. It will appear and reappear all through time.

57   Death

See also *Fear*.

Apart from the unpredictable time of the rapture[209], death is the one thing in life that no one can avoid. All the power, money, and influence in the world count for nothing when the time to die arrives for a person. Death is the great equalizer. Whatever the playing field during life, it is leveled for everyone at the end of their lives. No one is special enough or important enough to avoid it. Hebrews 9:27 (NIV) says, *Just as man is destined to die once, and after that to face judgment, ...*

Yet Jesus brought a different message—a message of amazing hope.

Jesus said to her, "I am the resurrection and the life. He who believes in me will live, even though he [physically] *dies; and whoever lives and believes in me will never* [spiritually] *die. ..."* (John 11:25-26, NIV, words in brackets added)

Paul gives a lengthy discourse about the resurrection of the

---
[209]   1 Corinthians 15:51-52

dead and our bodies in 1 Corinthians 15:12-58[210] that is worth reading. He prefers to refer to Christians that have already died as having *fallen asleep,* because he knows that some of his readers are mistaken about what death is like for Christians. Jesus himself explained clearly that at the resurrection believers will be like angels and can no longer die.[211]

Paul writes in 1 Thessalonians 5:23 (NIV), ... *May your whole spirit, soul and body be kept blameless at the coming of our Lord Jesus Christ.*

Typical American usage of the word *soul* refers to what this passage calls *spirit* and *soul*—the parts of you other than your body. It includes your knowledge, memory, thoughts, emotions, and your connection and relationship with God. It is an error to think these will disappear when your brain ceases to function. We have all been created spiritual beings with bodies.

Luke 16:19-31 is sometimes thought of as a parable, but it is not. Jesus told this narrative as something that actually happened. In this passage of the rich man and Lazarus (a different Lazarus than Jesus raised from the dead) we get a glimpse of what the afterlife was like before Christ died on the cross. The people there are having a conversation just like we normally have.

The strongest testimony of what our ultimate condition will be is demonstrated by Jesus after his resurrection. Jesus is called the *firstborn from the dead*, meaning that we are going to be reborn from the dead just as he was.[212] After the Father raised him from the dead, Jesus was just as he had been in terms of thinking and communicating. It will be the same for us.

There is nothing wrong with visualizing your death as like

---

210 *See also* 2 Corinthians 5:1-10
211 Luke 20:27-40 (*See also* Matthew 22:23-33, Mark 12:18-27)
212 Romans 8:29, Revelation 1:5

falling asleep and immediately[213] awaking in the presence of saved family that died before you and God with his wonderful, tangible love—feeling better than you ever have before, being full of joy, and having perfect clarity of thought, never again experiencing any loneliness, emptiness, or pain.

---

213 2 Corinthians 5:6-8

58   Fear

After eating the fruit forbidden by God in the Garden of Eden, the first effect described in Genesis 3 was that Adam and Eve realized they were naked. They had taken upon themselves the knowledge of good and evil, and the result was the knowledge that they had done evil. Their consciences convicted them of this fact, and as a (spiritually healthy) result, were *ashamed* and sewed fig leaves together to cover themselves.[214]

Immediately following we see that the first effect of the *presence* of God upon Adam and Eve was *fear*. The Bible uses the word *fear* in two ways. If a pack of lions jumped out of the tall grass and was going to attack, a kind of fear would arise that comes when **someone realizes he is not in control of his life and something may happen that he doesn't want to happen.** This is the kind of fear we are most familiar with.

The other kind of fear found in the Bible is the *fear of God*. It occurs when a heightened awareness of God invokes an *awe* and *reverence* of God in us. Physically, it can feel like the first kind

---
214 Genesis 3:7

of fear. There is a tangible effect of being in God's presence—a greater awareness of the contrast between the person, who has a sinful nature, and God's greatness and purity—his holiness. It is an experience that can invoke a powerful feeling of humility in us.[215] *This is a healthy response to God and his presence.*

The rest of this chapter is about the loss-of-control kind of fear.

Understanding why we might be afraid of something gives us insight into why we experience fear and also reveals avenues through which we might overcome it. It explains why we may be afraid of flying, of having someone point a gun at us, or of speaking in front of a hundred people. In all these cases we want to have more control of the situation, or the people involved, than we believe we will have. But why does fear point to a lack of control? It is because we want to prevent ourselves from being *hurt*.

If sin can be called the world's worst plague, fear might be called the plague's worst symptom. God does not want us to be afraid of anything. Sadly, in this fallen world, we spend part of our formative years experiencing various hurts and the fear of them. Some people are exposed to situations that cause fears that we were simply not designed to be able to handle. Children (of any age) are vulnerable because of their immaturity and innocence. Wartime soldiers are vulnerable because of how extreme their exposure can be. Our fears can give darkness an entry point into our psyche, and we can be affected into adulthood, and more often than we think, for the rest of our lives.

Determining someone's underlying sources of fear can be difficult. A Christian is only afraid when she does not *know* or does not *believe* the truth about God or herself. (Not believing the truth

---

[215] Isaiah 6:1-6

can also be understood as being deceived or having elements of spiritual blindness). Deceptions can be much deeper than intellectual misunderstandings. (See also *The Cross*.) God will sometimes reveal the source of our fears to us if we ask him. Other times God will reveal the truth through someone else sharing what they know, Bible study, over time through persistent prayer, or from working with a psychologist (preferably a Christian psychologist who believes in the present day power and involvement of Jesus Christ in our lives). Understanding what is causing one's fears gives one the opportunity to gain power over them.[216] Some fears disappear as God sanctifies us without our actively seeking freedom from them, but overcoming deeply rooted fears may require a more directed strategy.

The most important thing for someone (who is saved by God) to learn about fear is that there is **never any logical reason to be afraid**. Our loving God is completely in control of our lives and everything around us. Nothing is hidden from his sight,[217] and no matter what happens to us, we are unalterably destined to eternal happiness with him without any punishment. It can take a long time for our emotions to line up with that truth, but the rewards of fighting that battle yields wonderful fruit, even in this life.[218]

While pain can be anywhere from unpleasant to agonizing, in a Christian, it is not a sign of moral failure. While on earth, pain triggers an awareness in our fallen physical selves that we deserve punishment.[219] However, when we die we will leave our fallen bodies behind. Jesus Christ has received the punishment due us for all of our moral failures. We no longer need have a fear-

---
216 John 8:31-32
217 Hebrews 4:13
218 Philippians 4:6-7
219 Romans 2:14-15

ful expectation of judgment.[220] God's sanctification works these truths into our hearts and minds, and we can come to experience pain without its familiar darkness.[221]

Fear of death is at the root of all fears. One of the main reasons Jesus came to earth is ... *so that by his [Jesus'] death he might destroy him who holds the power of death—that is, the devil—* **and free those who all their lives were held in slavery by their fear of death.** (Hebrews 2:14-15, NIV, bold and text in brackets added)

We learn in 1 Corinthians 15:56 (NIV) that, *The sting of death is sin,* ... The reason that death is so awful is because it embodies separation from God. But for followers of Jesus Christ, all we will do for the rest of our lives and all eternity is *grow closer to God.*

Jesus taught in Matthew 10:28-31 that if we wanted someone to be afraid of, it would make more sense to be afraid of God, not afraid of Satan and his kingdom—but that there is no reason to be afraid of God. On the contrary, ...*God has said, "Never will I leave you; never will I forsake you." So we say with confidence, "The Lord is my helper; I will not be afraid. What can man do to me?"*[222] (Hebrews 13:5-6, NIV)

John 11:25-26 (NIV, words in brackets added): *Jesus said to her, "I am the resurrection and the life. He who believes in me will live, even though he [physically] dies; and whoever lives and believes in me will never [spiritually] die. Do you believe this?"*

While not being afraid of death and all its companion fears is a good goal to have, much of our fight is in trying to deal with

---

220 Hebrews 10:26-27
221 James 1:2, 1 Peter 1:3-7, 4:12-13
222 *See also* Psalms 23, 91, et al.

our fear of people and the things they might do. Regarding people who might actually be trying to kill his twelve apostles, Jesus' concluding command in Matthew 10:17-31 is *So do not be afraid of them.* (verse 26, NIV) The reason he gives can be interpreted as *stick to the truth; they won't get away with anything.* How much less we should fear people who do not threaten our lives. In fact, the Holy Spirit, though the apostle Paul, teaches us not to even be *anxious* about anything in Philippians 4:6 (NIV): *Do not be anxious about anything, but in everything, by prayer and petition, with thanksgiving, present your requests to God.*

59 Life

God designed humans to have perfect peace and satisfaction when we are in perfect harmony with God, as Adam and Eve were before the fall—and as Christians will be after we shed our fallen flesh. In our separation from God, our souls ache and have an emptiness that we can perceive. This spiritual emptiness is like physical hunger, except that with hunger we learned from an early age that food will temporarily satisfy it. Our current separation from God is an abnormal condition. Some people are more sensitive to this and have more painful lives. It can be difficult to function when something as essential as God's full presence is missing. This pain and emptiness is the part of us that moves us to seek spiritual peace.

This inner ache is what pushes us to grasp for the divine—looking for substitutes when the genuine is not fully experienced. It drives us to seek companionship, a sense of belonging, and approval. We look for resolution in relationships, sensual pleasures, gangs, and churches. Some try to numb the pain of it with pornography, alcohol/drugs, or living their lives at a pace that is as fast as they can manage. Materialism provides a salve to our soul that tells us we are worthy to be treated as special, as does what we can do with power. Some people try to find peace through much prayer or by making an extreme effort to be obedient to God. (See also *The Slipperiest Deceptions*.)

If what we try didn't help, we wouldn't do it anymore. But usually what we do does help, but only temporarily, then we are back to repeating whatever gave us temporary relief. A non-Christian spirituality can produce a longer lasting satisfaction than these, but in the end it will be found only to have been a better deception. Spirituality that offers easier and faster methods will also prove dry and empty in the end. None of these will satisfy the emptiness within us and give our souls peace and rest that lasts.

Remember that the Bible has a word for separation from God: *death*. It is perhaps not too much of a surprise that the aforementioned emptiness, dryness, and pains are actually small kinds of death—partial separation from God. The efforts to find peace and rest are efforts to find spiritual *Life*. Jesus said in John 10:10 (NIV), *I have come that they may have life, and have it to the full.*

The meaning of John 14:6 (NIV, bold added) may be a little clearer: *Jesus answered, "I am the way and the truth and the life...."* Attaining to the whole measure of the fullness Christ[223] is to achieve oneness with God and our fellow man[224] (See also *The Ancestral Connection* and *The Community Connection*.) There is no quick and easy path, and it is not something we can fully achieve in this life. However, it is something that God will give us rich portions of as we walk with him and get to know him bet-

---
223 Ephesians 4:13
224 John 17:21

ter.[225] Our experience of peace, rest, and satisfaction increases, and our experience of emptiness and separation decreases—as we blossom into the fullness of eternal life.

---

225   John 7:37-39

60 Potent Human Spiritual Power

Television shows, movies, and games are devoted to trying to invoke a feeling of power in us. Children and adults activate their powers with futuristic electronics or by exerting their will in a certain way. They fly, they direct huge blasts of destruction, they flick speeding locomotives away as if they were gnats.

These fantasies can be satisfying, but they grieve my soul, because they indicate that we as a nation and individuals feel starved of power. We look for, strive, and even suffer in the hope of destroying the obstacles in our lives. We want to brush them away—or at least want them to *just go away*. Consider the conflicts around the world. Nearly all of them can be attributed to individuals or groups of people who are not having their needs met and have decided to go to extremes to grasp for enough power to set things "right."

But Christians are not in the midst of an epidemic of powerlessness. We are in the midst of an epidemic of *perceived* powerlessness. The truth is that with Christ we have more than enough power to overcome *all* the obstacles in our lives[226]—but it will often require persistence and patience on our part. It will also require *believing God*—and obedience to God, because this is one of the ways that God alters the world around us. If a child wants to jump across a creek without getting wet, and his parent tells him he will need a running start, but the child ignores the advice, then the child may very well fail. God's commands and wisdom are of no use to someone who does not apply them.

While it is sometimes very difficult to accept, some obstacles require that we have *already* built a strong foundation in Christ.[227] It is not that we can not overcome such obstacles with God's help, but we may reach a place where God decides it is best for us to experience the natural consequences of not having built a firm enough foundation. All things are possible for him who believes[228], but sometimes persistence is required. What happens if we do not persist?

James 5:16-18 (NIV) says, ... *The prayer of a righteous man is powerful and effective. Elijah was a man just like us. He prayed earnestly that it would not rain, and it did not rain on the land for three and a half years. Again he prayed, and the heavens gave rain, and the earth produced its crops.*

We are appropriately taught that prayer is a powerful part of our arsenal for dealing with obstacles in our lives.[229] It is one way

---
226 John 16:33, 1 John 5:5
227 Matthew 7:24-27
228 Matthew 19:26, Mark 9:23, Luke 18:27
229 Ephesians 6:18

that we can bring God's help to bear on the problem. But we have another potent spiritual power. It may not seem spectacular, and can be rather unexciting to hear about.

The physical realm and the spiritual realm are connected. In fact it may be more accurate not to suggest that they are separate, but rather that they are two ways of looking at our reality. What happens in the spiritual affects the physical—that is why the effects of prayer are experienced on earth. Prayer is not *just* talking to God, it also is a way of changing the spiritual and physical with God's help.

In the same way, our earthly actions affect the spiritual realm. Our lives can be living prayers to God.[230] When we physically perform a good deed, the spiritual is also affected. When we choose to follow a command of God in the physical, the spiritual is also changed.[231]

If you want to bring all the power available to you to bear on a problem in your life, be both persistent in prayer[232] and persistent in **Christlike action**. Get other people to pray with you and for you—and *get them to help you in the physical*. If health permits, include a little fasting in your weekly regimen.[233] The results can be miraculous. *Nothing will be impossible for you.* (Matthew 17:20, NIV)

---

[230] 1 Thessalonians 5:17
[231] Romans 12:1
[232] Matthew 7:7-11
[233] Matthew 6:18 (*Father...will reward you*)

61 Time Is Short

In 1865 the 13th constitutional amendment was ratified and slavery became illegal in the United States. In 1868 the 14th amendment allowed former slaves to become United States citizens, and in 1870 the 15th amendment disallowed race as a factor in qualifying to vote.

So, racial prejudice in the United States ended in 1870, right?

Practices in some Southern states prevented some African-Americans from voting until *1965* when the Voting Rights Act was passed. Major social change is slow. *Very slow.* You can still find the effects of slavery on a vast scale in American culture 140 years later. It is probably going to be *at least* several hundred more years before the cultural effects of slavery in the United States have mostly disappeared.

Jesus says he is coming soon—*time is short.*[234] Do you believe it? Consider how much work there is for Christians to do on earth and *how long that work takes transform a culture.* The work you do today will not be complete in its effects for a very long time

---
234   1 Corinthians 7:29, 31, Revelation 3:11, 12:12, 22:7, 12, 20

by a typical human standard of time. Considered another way: the work you do or do not do today will affect the eternal destination of people that will not be born for another three hundred years. You only have your lifetime to help those people—*your* time to help them is short.

Do not minimize your work for the Lord, though it may appear to be a small thing. You do not have to participate in a worldwide ministry for the effects of your work to last hundreds of years. Saying a kind word to someone who is sad can move mountains. There is a spiritual aspect to following Jesus Christ that has mysterious effects. Jesus states a spiritual law in John 12:24—he compares an action for God to a tiny kernel of wheat—that it produces more kernels of wheat. God grants future blessings based on even small actions that please him for thousands of years![235]

---

235   Deuteronomy 5:8-10

62 You Can Take It With You

Fortunately for us, there are quite a number of things that Christians in a right relationship with God get to take with us to heaven. In fact the most important thing in our lives can be taken with us: our relationship with God. Whatever its condition, it continues without interruption when we die.

Something else we take with us when we die is our history. Everything we have ever done and said (and not done and not said) remains unchanged by our passage through death. (Our sins were wiped away when we repented of them.)

We will also be taking with us our knowledge and the glory given to us by God. And while we cannot strictly say we will be taking it with us, the heavenly treasure we have worked for while on earth will be waiting for us.

The desire to take financial wealth to heaven is not entirely misguided. There is nothing wrong with wanting to be comfortable and happy in heaven, for example. However any good thing we might want money for will be given to us without cost. We will be given a dwelling and also excellent friends (better than our best earthly family and friend relationships). In fact we will experience the benefits of being co-owners of *everything*[236].

One thing we will not take with us is our fallen bodies. (The older or sicker you are, the more likely you are happy to hear that.) From the beginning, God intended that humans should have bodies (unlike spiritual beings such as angels) on earth, and our death does not change that. We will receive resurrected, transformed, immortal bodies that are not tainted by sin[237] and we will eventually dwell on a new, unfallen earth. Our bodies will truly be holy and pure. Our sin nature, all sin, and the effects of all sin will be utterly gone forever.

---

236   1 Corinthians 3:21-23
237   1 Corinthians 15:35-58

63 The Master Plan

Mark 4:14-20 (NIV): *"The farmer sows the word. Some people are like seed along the path, where the word is sown. As soon as they hear it, Satan comes and takes away the word that was sown in them. Others, like seed sown on rocky places, hear the word and at once receive it with joy. But since they have no root, they last only a short time. When trouble or persecution comes because of the word, they quickly fall away. Still others, like seed sown among thorns, hear the word; but the worries of this life, the deceitfulness of wealth and the desires for other things come in and choke the word, making it unfruitful. Others, like seed sown on good soil, hear the word, accept it, and produce a crop—thirty, sixty or even a hundred times what was sown."*

When sharing our faith with someone, wouldn't it be great if we were able to prevent Satan from stealing the word that we sowed, ensure the truths we shared had sufficient root—and made sure they were not choked by contrary experiences going on in that person's life?

Not only that, but wouldn't it be fantastic if such an evangelist did not forget about that person after the testimony about his faith was accepted, but first ensured he became connected to a church that would continue to meet his needs?

And wouldn't it be amazing if the individuals at that church took it upon themselves to make sure that person's minimal material needs were met, and generously met their spiritual needs, such as the knowledge of God, Bible study, and personal holiness?

What a great plan this would be for saving people from eternal suffering and instead destining them for great and glorious things! If the individuals at the church also helped Christians to be evangelists, then the church would be self-propagating—that is, those that were saved would eventually become people that helped save other people.

What a masterful plan! The growth of the number of followers of Jesus Christ would be exponential! I wish someone had thought of this before!

Well, someone did. Matthew 28:18-20 (NIV, bold added): *Then Jesus came to them and said, "All authority in heaven and on earth has been given to me. Therefore go and **make disciples** of all nations, baptizing them in the name of the Father and of the Son and of the Holy Spirit, and teaching them to obey everything I have commanded you. ..."*

64 Discerning the Genuine

The time is upon us when false miracles will be used to "prove" things other than Jesus Christ alone is Lord. God, through various people in the Bible, including Jesus, told us to *keep watch* and *beware*. Watch out for prophetic people that are not from God.[238] Watch out that no one deceives you about who Jesus is.[239]

God has given us the knowledge to continue to move forward in our devotion to him and avoid what is contrary to God, as well. Matthew 7:17-18 (NIV, bold added) says, *Likewise every good tree bears good fruit, but a bad tree bears bad fruit. A good tree **cannot** bear bad fruit, and a bad tree **cannot** bear good fruit.*

As you walk with God, your ability to discern good from evil will get better. Paul gives us good examples of what bad fruit is in Galatians 5:19-21 (NIV): *The acts of the sinful nature are obvious: sexual immorality, impurity and debauchery; idolatry and*

---
238 Mathew 7:15-16
239 Mark 13:5-6

Discerning the Genuine

witchcraft; hatred, discord, jealousy, fits of rage, selfish ambition, dissensions, factions and envy; drunkenness, orgies, and the like. ... Some of these may be rare, but watch out for the ones that are not uncommon in our culture, such as idolatry, discord, jealousy, and selfish ambition. Remember that our adversary, Satan, is very real, and can masquerade as an angel.[240] He deceives so sins are made to be fun, enjoyable, and pleasing—but will only pull you deeper into sin, and sin will *always* take you farther than you ever intended to go.

Paul also teaches what the fruits of the Holy Spirit are in Galatians 5:22-23 (NIV): *But the fruit of the Spirit is love, joy, peace, patience, kindness, goodness, faithfulness, gentleness and self-control. Against such things there is no law.*

John, the Baptist said in Luke 3:8 (NIV), *Produce fruit in keeping with repentance. ...* and goes on to help people understand what that meant in verses 10-14.

In Ephesians 4:2-3 (NIV), Paul says, *Be completely humble and gentle; be patient, bearing with one another in love. Make every effort to keep the unity of the Spirit through the bond of peace.* Learn what the *unity of the Spirit* is like so you can recognize when it is present and when it is absent.

If the root of something is evil, it will bring forth separation from Jesus Christ[241]. A bad tree can only bear bad fruit, but it may look like good fruit along the way. Because of this, it is important to have access to Godly church elders. Godly church elders will not be controlling and will not think they have a monopoly on the truth. They will be trusting God in many ways. They will be trying to follow God, not lead him. When they are under pressure,

---

240 2 Corinthians 11:14
241 Romans 6:23

they will still demonstrate the fruits of the Spirit.

The most important safeguard is to study the Bible yourself under the guidance of competent people. There are bits and pieces of wisdom for discerning what is from God and what is not all throughout Scripture. Spend part of (or a lot of) your time learning from God himself.[242] Think and pray about the meaning of what you have read in the Bible instead of just listening to what other people say. In John 16:13 (NIV) Jesus said, *...when he, the Spirit of truth, comes, he will guide you into all truth. ...*

---

[242] Matthew 23:10, Colossians 3:16, Hebrews 8:10, 10:16

65 The End Times, For Us

See also *Discerning The Genuine*.

In these end times, the Lord is going to drive the members of the body, his church, together, because it is only together that we can stand against the devil's worst schemes. If you are mostly aware of the devil's work against individuals (sickness, divorce, etc.), you need to know that he also has schemes for churches, communities, and families that cannot be overcome by individuals walking in the power of God.[243] (See also The Community Connection.)

You may have never been *tossed back and forth by the waves, and blown here and there by every wind of teaching and by the cunning and craftiness of men in their deceitful scheming* (Ephesians 4:14, NIV) You also may not have been aware of being subject to the power of evil spirits (since Satan is the father of all

---
243   Ezekiel 14:20, Mark 6:5. Also 14:12-23.

deceitful scheming.) If not, you probably cannot appreciate the value in no longer being an infant in Christ. Being blown about with no foundation to hold onto is a horrible experience and usually lasts quite a while. It is the church's responsibility to protect these people until they have grown up in Christ. (But they can do little if the person they are trying to help refuses to do what they suggest.)

As the Ephesians passage says, the church is ... *to prepare God's people for **works of service**, so that the body of Christ may be built up until we all reach **unity in the faith** and in the knowledge of the Son of God and become mature, attaining to the whole measure of the fullness of Christ.* (Ephesians 4:12-13, NIV, bold added)

It is essential that individuals, small groups, churches, ministries, and communities be founded on the only foundation that works: the foundation of Jesus Christ **himself**.[244] Not what he was like, not his philosophy of being forgiving and giving, and not even Scripture. The only foundation that always works is the foundation of the real, living person, Jesus Christ, the Son of God.

It doesn't matter who the miracle worker is, who is prophesying, who is handing out food at the homeless shelter, or who is called an elder. Each person needs to seek God to find his place in the body. You will receive more joy and eternal reward doing what God made you to do, even if it is vacuuming the church carpet each week, than if you had a more visible, so-called honorable role. Remember, the more responsibility you have, the greater the "weight of the world" you must successfully carry. Such people have greater accountability to God.[245]

---

244 1 Corinthians 3:11
245 Matthew 25:14-30

Do not let your head dwell in the clouds, where other people are watching for which human is the Anti-Christ. Do not put your faith in your preparations for catastrophe. Dig into your Bible with your friends and talk about God with them. Talk more with God and strive to better understand what he is doing in your life—he has a purpose for everyone.[246] Ask him questions about himself. Do good works where he has put you—the kinds of things you have training or talent for and can do, not the tasks you see other people doing in your church or in the Bible. These are the most powerful ways to open the doors that will allow God to cover your entire life with protection and blessings.

---

[246] Ephesians 2:10

Final Thought:

"Therefore I tell you, do not worry about your life, what you will eat or drink; or about your body, what you will wear. Is not life more important than food, and the body more important than clothes? Look at the birds of the air; they do not sow or reap or store away in barns, and yet your heavenly Father feeds them. Are you not much more valuable than they? Who of you by worrying can add a single hour to his life?

"And why do you worry about clothes? See how the lilies of the field grow. They do not labor or spin. Yet I tell you that not even Solomon in all his splendor was dressed like one of these. If that is how God clothes the grass of the field, which is here today and tomorrow is thrown into the fire, will he not much more clothe you, O you of little faith? So do not worry, saying, 'What shall we eat?' or 'What shall we drink?' or 'What shall we wear?' For the pagans run after all these things, and your heavenly Father knows that you need them. But seek first his kingdom and his righteousness, and all these things will be given to you as well. Therefore do not worry about tomorrow, for tomorrow will worry about itself. Each day has enough trouble of its own." (Jesus speaking in Matthew 6:25-34, NIV)

"Do not let your hearts be troubled. Trust in God; trust also in me." (Jesus speaking in John 14:1, NIV)

See *www.god-colored.com* for errata and other information.

About The Author

The author was born in 1963 and was raised in Champaign, Illinois. He received his Bachelors of Science in 1985 in Computer Science and Mathematics from the University of Illinois at Urbana-Champaign. For much of his professional career he worked for software development consulting companies primarily involved in computer-based education and training.

In 1992, he was led to read the Bible to find out what this Jesus he had heard of was really like. Finding the Bible very interesting reading, he read an hour an evening for a year. This Bible reading along with a tape series entitled The Reliability of the Gospels by Andy Stanley caused him to conclude that the Bible could not have been written by humans alone. He came to a firm decision to be a follower of Jesus Christ in 1993. Afterward he started watching Baptist preacher Charles Stanley's televised sermons. The foundation of the author's theological views came directly from that first year of Bible reading, and was added to and bolstered by Charles Stanley's teaching.

The author was eventually led to look for a church home, and attended a Catholic church for a short while, as he had done in his youth, but did not find it sufficiently alive with the spirit of God. He settled on an Assembly of God church where God had led him and where he found the theology consistent with Scripture, and attended it for nine years.

After relocating to be nearer to his family, the author became a member of one of the churches in the Vineyard Fellowship, where he still attends.

The author has had an eventful life—with events such as cancer and the permanent effects of radiation; progressive hearing loss; decades of social anxiety disorder and its accompanying constant fear; a lifetime of depression with 10 years of being sufficiently disabled to be unable to work; one and a half years of unmedicated bipolar disorder II (this was as bad as everything else combined); and more than a decade of intense loneliness, the worst of which evaporated at the moment he made a decision to follow Jesus Christ.

The author is happy most of the time now.

www.ingramcontent.com/pod-product-compliance
Lightning Source LLC
Chambersburg PA
CBHW031244290426
44109CB00012B/427